MELTDOWN MANAGEMENT: STRATEGIES TO HANDLE

Meltdowns in Children with Autism and Special Needs

Kathryn Paddington

© Copyright 2019 - All rights reserved.

It is not legal to reproduce, duplicate, or transmit any part of this document in either electronic means or in printed format. Recording of this publication is strictly prohibited and any storage of this document is not allowed unless with written permission from the publisher except for the use of brief quotations in a book review.

Get the Letter of Intent FOR FREE.

Sign up for the no-spam newsletter, and get the LETTER OF INTENT for free.

Details can be found at the end of the book.

The author and publisher have provided this e-book to you for your personal use only. You may not make this e-book publicly available in any way. Copyright infringement is against the law. If you believe the copy of this e-book you are reading infringes on the author's copyright, please notify us at diffnotless.com/piracy

Table of Contents

Chapter 1
Meltdowns 1
   a. Introduction 1
   b. Facts about Tantrums and Meltdowns 4
   c. Anatomy of a Sensory Meltdown 5
   d. Causes of Meltdowns 6
     i. Underlying causes 6
       1. Attention-deficit/hyperactivity disorder 7
       2. Unease 7
       3. Learning complications 8
       4. Depression and irritability 8
       5. Autism spectrum disorder 8
       6. Sensory processing problems 9
     ii. Lack of certain skills. 9
   e. Difference between Temper Tantrums and Meltdowns 9
   f. Meltdowns, Tantrums, and Aggression 12
   g. Telling The Difference Between A Sensory Meltdown Vs. Temper Tantrum 13
     i. The intensity of the tantrum. 13
     ii. Length of a meltdown before calming down. 13
     iii. Frequency of the tantrums and their persistence 13
   h. How Autistic Meltdowns Differ from Ordinary Temper Tantrums 14
   i. Qualities of an Autistic Meltdown 14
       1. Meltdowns are not limited to children 15
       2. Meltdowns are heralded by signs of distress 15
       3. Meltdowns may involve intense stimming 15
       4. Meltdowns do not have a purpose 16
   j. How Autistic Symptoms Relate to Meltdowns 16

v

    k. Managing Autistic Meltdowns 16
    l. The Challenges of Meltdown Mismanagements 17
      i. Paying undue attention to a tantrum. 18
      ii. Reassuring the child during a tantrum. 19
      iii. Giving in to the child's demands. 19
      iv. Repeatedly issuing warning to the child. 19
      v. Paying off the child. 20

Chapter 2
A Closer Look at Meltdowns 21
    a. Stages in Meltdowns for Toddlers 21
      i. Denial. 21
      ii. Anger. 21
      iii. Bargaining. 22
      iv. Depression. 22
      v. Acceptance. 22
    b. Stages in Meltdowns for Children with ASD and Other
    Special Needs 22
      i. The buildup phase. 23
      ii. The meltdown/shutdown phase. 25
      iii. Recovery phase. 25
    c. The Meltdown Cycle 26
    d. The Cycle of Tantrums, Rage, and Meltdowns 28
      i. The rumbling stage. 28
        1. Antiseptic bouncing. 29
        2. Proximity control 29
        3. Signal interference 30
        4. Support from routine 30
        5. Just walk, and don't talk 31
        6. Redirecting 31
        7. Home base 31
      ii. Rage stage. 33
      iii. Recovery stage. 34
    e. Triggers for Meltdowns in Children with Autism Spectrum
    Disorder 35
      i. Unexpected routine changes. 36

ii. Loud sounds or excessive noise... 36
  iii. Overwhelming feeling in a new environment. 37
  iv. Crowded places. 37
  v. Unattended needs. 38
  vi. When people aren't on your level. 38
  vii. Sensory overload. 38
  viii. Unambiguous or trivial triggers. 39
  ix. When things feel unbridled. 39
  x. Feeling locked in. 39
  xi. Uncomfortable social interactions. 40
 f. Understanding Sensory Implications for Meltdowns 40
 g. Sensory Thresholds... 42
 h. Parental Strategies for Helping with Sensory Thresholds... 42
  i.   Be observant and sensitive to the sensory thresholds of the child... 42
  ii. Recognize how the child responds when approaching their sensory threshold. 44
  iii. Identify what behavior to anticipate in the child when they reach their sensory threshold. 45
  iv.   Pinpoint what works best for relieving the child from a meltdown. 45
  v.   Give the child a sensory diet... 46
  i. Sensory Questions 47

Chapter 3
Managing Meltdowns 49
 a. Self-Regulation 49
  i. Self-regulation is a cerebral process that originates from infancy. 50
  ii. Self-regulation is an executive function of the brain. 51
  iii. Self-regulation is entwined with emotional development. 51
  iv. Self-regulation is entwined with social development. 51
 b. Why Self-Regulation Is Important 51
 c. How and When Self-Regulation Develops.......................... 52
 d. Self-Regulation Theory 53

    d. Self-Regulated Learning...54
    e. The Psychology of Self-Regulation 55
    f. Self-Regulation Therapy 56
    g. Appreciating Ego Depletion 57
    h. The Importance of Self-Regulation................................58
       i. Emotional intelligence. 59
       ii. Motivation to succeed. 60
       iii. Attention-Deficit/Hyperactivity Disorder and Autism......60
    i. The Art of Mindfulness 62
    j. Executive Function..63
    k. Self-Regulation Test and Assessment 64

Chapter 4
Managing Meltdowns Continued 66
    a. Early Childhood and Child Development........................66
    b. Teaching and Developing Self-Regulation in Toddlers........66
    c. Games for Teaching and Developing Self-Regulation in Kindergarten and Preschool Children 67
       i. Red Light, Green Light. 68
       ii. Mother, May I?..68
       iii. Freeze Dance..68
       iv. Follow My Clap..68
       v. Loud or Quiet. 68
       vi. Simon Says. 69
       vii. Body Part Mix-Up...69
       viii. Follow the Leader..69
       ix. Ready, Set, Wiggle. 70
       x. Color Moves. 70
       xi. Classic games. 70
    d. Self-Regulation in Adolescence 71
    e. The Role of Self-Regulation in Education 72
    f. Strategies, Exercises, and Lesson Plans for Students in the Classroom 73
       i. McGill self-regulation lesson plans...............................73
       ii. College and career competency framework and lessons..74
    g. Self-Regulation in Adults 75

h. Cognitive Reappraisal 77
i. Skills and Techniques to Improve Self-Regulation in Adults 77
   1.   Leading and living with integrity 77
   2.   Being open to change 78
   3.   Identify your triggers 78
   4.   Practicing self-discipline 78
   5.   Reframe negative thoughts 79
   6.   Keep calm under pressure 79
   7.   Consider the consequences 79
   8.   Believe in yourself 79
j. Self-Regulation Strategies: Methods for Managing Oneself 80
k. Emotion Regulation Skills 81
l. Self-Regulation Chart and Checklist 82
m. Teaching Self-Regulation in the Classroom 84
   i. Make rules and expectations abundantly clear. 84
   ii. Employ the use of visual schedules. 84
   ii. Concentrate positive reinforcement. 85
   iii. Teach calming tactics 85
   1. Practice deep breathing 86
   2. Use rewards 86
   3. Make a calm down box 86
   4. Cultivate a "calm down corner" 87
   5. Make transitions slowly 87
n. The Zones of Self-Regulation 87
o. The Colors in the Zones of Regulation Program 88
p. Zones of Regulation Activities 92
   1. Zones pocket play for emotions and coping approaches folders 93
   2. Zone check-in tubes 93
   3. Zone check-in frames 94
   4. Zone grab bag game 94
   5. Zones of regulation craft 95
   6. Coping skills toolbox 95
   7. Zone of regulation chart 96
q. Keep a Self-Reflection Journal 96

    r. Identify Emotions through Play 97
    s. Explore Self-regulation Skills 98

Chapter 5
Managing Tantrums 99
    a. Anatomy of a Temper Tantrum 99
    b. How to Manage and Prevent a Temper Tantrum 99
        Rule One: It's not about you 100
        Rule Two: Define the motivation for the tantrums 100
    c. Causes of Temper Tantrums 100
        i. An emotional sneeze. 101
        ii. Temper tantrums in public. 101
        iii. Write a story. 102
        Rule Three: Breathe 102
    d. Sensory Integration Tools for Meltdown Management 103
    e. The Role of Self-Regulation 103
    f. Sensory Integration Toolkits 103
    g. When Away from Home 104
    h. When at Home 105
    i. When at Playdates and in School 106

Chapter 6
Managing Panic Attacks 107
    a. How to Manage and Prevent a Panic Attack 107
    b. Panic Attack Symptoms 108
    c. When to See a Doctor 109
    d. Causes of Panic Attack 109
    e. Risk Factors 110
    f. Complications 111
    g. Prevention 112
    h. Ways to Stop a Panic Attack 112
        i. Employ deep breathing. 112
        ii. Be aware of the imminent panic attack. 113
        iii. Close eyes. 113
        iv. Practice mindfulness. 113
        v. Find a focus object. 114
        vi. Employ muscle relaxation techniques. 114

- vii. Picture a happy place. 114
- viii. Engage in light exercise. 115
- ix. Keep lavender on hand. 115
- x. Repeat a mantra internally. 115
- xi. Take benzodiazepines. 116
- i. Cognitive-Behavioral Therapy 116
- j. Types of Cognitive-Behavioral Therapy 117
  - i. Behavior therapy. 117
  - ii. Cognitive therapy. 118
  - iii. Cognitive-behavioral therapy. 118
  - iv. Acceptance and commitment therapy. 119
  - v. Dialectical behavior therapy. 120
  - vi. Functional analytic psychotherapy. 121
  - vii. Compassion informed psychotherapy. 121
  - viii. Mindfulness-based cognitive therapy. 122
  - ix. Integrative couples behavior therapy. 122
- k. What to Expect During a Cognitive-Behavioral Therapy Session 123
- l. Techniques Used With Cognitive-Behavioral Therapy 125
  - i. Cognitive restructuring or reframing 126
  - ii. Guided discovery 126
  - iii. Exposure therapy 126
  - iv. Journaling and thought records. 127
  - v. Activity scheduling and behavior activation. 127
  - vi. Behavioral experiments. 127
  - vii. Relaxation and stress reduction techniques. 128
  - viii. Role-playing. 128
- m. What Cognitive-Behavioral Therapy Can Help With 129
- n. Benefits. 130
- o. Effectiveness. 131
- p. Things to Consider 132
  - i. Difficulty in changing. 133
  - ii. The rigid structure of cognitive-behavioral therapy. ... 133
  - iii. The willingness to change. 133
  - iv. Gradual progress. 133

- q. Things to Keep in Mind 134
  - i. It's not a cure. 134
  - ii. Results take time. 134
  - iii. It isn't always fun. 134
  - iv. It's just one of many options. 135
- r. How to Get Started 135
  - i. Calm the nervous system. 136
  - ii. Create an ingenious plan. 137
  - iii. Persist in the face of obstacles and failure. 137
  - iv. Evaluate and adjust the plan. 138
- s. Agoraphobia 138
- t. Symptoms of Agoraphobia 139
- u. Panic Disorder and Agoraphobia 140
- v. When to See a Doctor 141
- w. Causes of Agoraphobia 141
- x. Risk Factors 142
- y. Complications 142
- z. Prevention 143
- aa. Prevention Summary 143
  - i. Preventing temper tantrums. 143
  - ii. Preventing sensory meltdowns. 144
  - iii. Preventing panic attacks. 144

Chapter 7
Sensory-Friendly Planning 145
- a. Tips for Planning a Sensory-Friendly Birthday Party 145
  - i. Use a theme your child likes. 145
  - ii. Have your guests in mind. 145
  - iii. Find a familiar location. 146
  - iv. Choose favorite activities. 146
  - v. An alternative to treats. 146
  - vi. Accepting gifts. 147
  - vii. Celebrate without a party. 147

Chapter 8
Instant Calm for the Extra Anxious 148
- a. How to Calm Down When Feeling Extra Anxious 148

    i. Breathe deeply. 148
    ii. Employ logic in challenging your fears. 149
    iii. Move your body... 150
    iv. Chew gum. 150
    v. Take a bath. 150
    vi. Go outside. 150
    vii. Write it out... 151
    viii. Sit up straight. 151
    ix. Listen to music. 152
    x. Think about what you're thankful for. 152
    xi. Close your eyes. 152
    xii. Play with your pet. 152
    xiii. Tense your toes and then relax them. 153
    xiv. Completely relax your muscles. 153
    xv. Watch something that makes you laugh. 153
    xvi. Smell something calming. 153
    xvii. Focus on a mantra.. 154
    xviii. Meditate. 154
  b. When It Might Be Something More 154
Get the Letter of Intent for Free 156
Found This Book Useful? 158
You Can Make a Big Difference 158

Chapter 1

Meltdowns

a. Introduction

Statistically, emotional outbursts such as tantrums and meltdowns are some of the most common challenges that bring young kids to the attention of a psychologist. Without a doubt, tantrums and meltdowns rank among some of the biggest challenges faced by parents today. This is partly because they are hard to fathom, hard to avert, and even harder to confront and manage effectively once they begin to manifest. In addition, when they ensue with the rate of recurrence that is past the age in which they're developmentally probable, they can turn out to be a big problem for the child, not just the struggling adults who stomach them.

So what is a meltdown?

We can describe a meltdown as a passionate reaction to any situation that the child considers as being overwhelming. It is an intense rejoinder to sensory overthrow. A meltdown occurs when a child becomes astounded by their present circumstances and for the time being loses control of their behavior. We can express this loss of control in a number of ways: from verbal such as yelling, screaming, and crying to physical such as thrusting, lashing out, and biting, or both.

A meltdown is categorically different from a temper tantrum or the exhibition of naughty behavior. When a child is utterly astounded, and their circumstance implies that it is tough to express themselves in any other way, they understandably resort to having a meltdown. Typically, meltdowns are not the only way a child articulates their feelings of being astounded. They may also choose to stop interacting, pull out from circumstances that they find perplexing, or circumvent them altogether.

For children with ASD and other special needs, once they are stunned, they know no other way to express their displeasure other than with a meltdown. This might comprise emotional verbal flare-ups such as screaming and crying, or physical reactions such as kicking, biting, or hitting. A lot of different things engender tantrums and meltdowns, from fright to frustration, irritation, or sensory overload, to name a few; this makes it exceptionally hard to understand how to go about managing them; and managing tantrums and meltdowns begins from first understanding how they occur, are sustained, and so on. Often, parents are confused about what's driving the behavior in their child when they begin to exhibit a tantrum or a meltdown. This is because these nasty displays aren't straightforward ways of effective communication, even though they may be powerful ways to get attention.

It's convenient to consider a meltdown as a response to a situation that a child can't handle in a more grown-up fashion such as by talking about their feelings, or explaining the authenticity of their wants, or simply doing what they are asked to do. But instead, the child is overawed by their emotions; the general thought of children at the threshold of such an outpour is that if allowing their feelings to run free in dramatic fashion—crying, screaming, kicking the floor, striking the wall, or hitting a parent—helps to get them what they want, then it's a behavior worth exploring to the very end.

This further implies that tantrums and meltdowns, even though not regarded as being consciously willful, or even voluntary are learned responses adopted by the child. A workable solution would mean exploring ways and methods that would encourage the child to unlearn such a response and instead learn other, more mature behaviors to handle a problem situation, such as meeting halfway or acting in accordance with parental instructions in exchange for some positive reward.

All children get irritated now and again. A meltdown can embody an extreme, angry outburst. They are typically seen in children between the ages of one and four.

- The child might yell, cry, roll on the floor, toss things, or stamp their feet.

- The child might hold their breath and turn red.

- The child might display general frustration, which is usually the basis of the meltdown.

- The child might go into a meltdown to get attention, get something they want, or avoid doing something.

- The child is likely to have a meltdown when they are hungry or tired.

- The child's meltdown may typically last less than fifteen minutes.

b. Facts about Tantrums and Meltdowns

- Tantrums and meltdowns are a common behavior in children from two to four years of age. This does not, however, excuse its occurrence and must be handled adequately by the parents.

- While frustrating to the parent, these behaviors echo the child's typical desire for freedom combined with the neurological naivety (such as communicative language skills) found in this age range.

- Parents can meritoriously manage these behaviors by keeping their composure and objectivity, and by not rewarding such behaviors no matter what. Walking away from the child during the tantrum or meltdown, for instance, shows the child that their tactic is ineffective. Another effective tool parents can effectively use is giving a time-out.

- Various approaches can be used to assist in the prevention of tantrums and meltdowns. Some of these approaches include having realistic behavioral expectations, allowing the child to make some choices in their everyday activities, and intentionally keeping an eye out and rewarding good behavior choices.

- Awfully frequent and disproportionately long-lasting tantrums, which last greater than five minutes and which involve violence particularly focused on younger siblings or other children, or parental sense of loss of control should trigger the need for an appointment with the child's pediatrician.

c. Anatomy of a Sensory Meltdown

A sensory meltdown is distinct from other hyperresponses. Sensory sensitivity to noise, lights, crowds, or touch can trigger children and adults who have sensory processing disorders to become disordered and frightened. The overloaded senses may lead to reactions that parents perceive as behavioral complications when they are just signs of sensory overload. Sensory meltdowns are not social interactions like tantrums. The child seldom cares whether anyone pays them any attention. The meltdown is also improbable to vanish as soon as the parent meets the need. In its place, it will subside slowly after the offensive stimulus has been removed. Even people who are not on the autism spectrum would probably respond to such overloaded senses. It's a frightening experience that flouts explanation to the person living with sensitivities.

d. Causes of Meltdowns

A meltdown is a rejoinder to an overpowering experience. It is important to identify what is overwhelming your child if they begin to have meltdowns. The best way to get an accurate analysis of what overwhelms your child is to keep and complete a diary over a period. This means you will keep a record of what happened before, during, and after each meltdown, tracking them to catch patterns. Tracking will help in discovering why the meltdowns arise at certain times, in certain places, or when something particular has happened.

i. Underlying causes. A child's view of the world is egocentric; they always want what they want when they want it. This self-absorbed view of their world is combined with a partial and lopsided development of expressive language skills when paralleled with their more complete receptive language skills, as the receptive language of a two-year-old child is numbered in the thousands, while the expressive skill generally is 150 to 200 words. A likely provoking truth for the child is their receptive ability to fathom complex sentence structures while only being able to express their thoughts in two- or three-word phrases.

A child's world is full of exploration and discovery; they largely have many skills and little judgment and learn by observation and repetitive trials. When a parent's desire for safety and limiting chaos clashes with the child's ferocious struggle for independence and the child's limited language capabilities, tantrums and meltdowns are almost inevitable.

When children don't cultivate emotional regulation as part of their typical development, the causes of tantrums and meltdowns are extensively varied. So tantrums and meltdowns can be triggered by a lot of distinct challenges that one cannot make them stop until an understanding of what is triggering them is gotten. Often, failing to regulate emotions results from an underlying problem. Some of the common causes of frequent meltdowns include the following:

1. *Attention-deficit/hyperactivity disorder*

   A recent study showed that over 75 percent of children who were seen to show severe temper outbursts also fit the benchmarks for attention-deficit/hyperactivity disorder (ADHD). That doesn't automatically imply that someone has medically diagnosed them with ADHD; the disorder may be overlooked in children who have a history of violence. A lack of attention and an inability to complete work and put up with boredom, among other symptoms, can underwrite the boom toward the explosive outbursts. So the underlying cause must be determined.

2. *Unease*

   Unease is another major contributor to meltdowns. Even if the child doesn't have a full-blown anxiety disorder, they may still be overreactive to circumstances that provoke unease, which could ultimately lead to a meltdown whenever they are anxious. Children who have undiagnosed learning disabilities or who have experienced trauma or neglect may retort this way when confronted with a bumpy or painful situation.

3. Learning complications

When a child acts out time after time in school or during homework time, they likely have an undiagnosed learning disorder. Say the child has a lot of trouble with math, and the subject makes them very upset and ill-tempered. Rather than asking for assistance, the child might rip up an assignment or start something with another child to fashion out a diversion from their real issues.

4. Depression and irritability

Children who have severe and frequent temper tantrums and meltdowns might have these experiences stem from depression and irritability. A new disorder called disruptive mood dysregulation disorder (DMDD) labels children who have severe outbursts with chronic severe irritability in between. A highly irritable child is like water at 90 degrees, always with a high likelihood of boiling over. Parents of such children are forced to be extra careful when dealing with them, as such kids respond to very subtle things, such as the slightest thing not going their way.

5. Autism spectrum disorder

Children on the spectrum are also often susceptible to dramatic meltdowns. This isn't surprising, as children with ASD tend to be unyielding and are dependent on a steady routine for their emotional comfort, with any unforeseen changes setting them off very quickly. In addition, they may likely lack the language and communication skills to express what they want or need.

6. Sensory processing problems

Sensory processing challenges, every so often displayed in children and teens with ASD and ADHD, may cause kids to be overwhelmed by stimulation and short-circuit in despairing meltdowns.

ii. Lack of certain skills. Regardless of the trigger, a lot of mental health professionals are of the opinion that children who have recurrent emotional outbursts are deficient in certain skills that would help them better manage circumstances that cause them frustration, nervousness, or anger. Some of these skills include the following:

- problem-solving
- impulse control
- negotiating
- self-soothing
- communicating wishes and needs to adults
- knowing what's appropriate or expected in a given situation
- delaying gratification

e. Difference between Temper Tantrums and Meltdowns

Even though neither tantrum nor meltdown is a clinical term, a lot of people make a distinction between the two behaviors. Tantrum is regularly used in the description of milder outbursts, during which a child still retains some measure of control over their behavior; it is usually a child's method for getting what they want. Tantrums almost always subside or fade off once no one pays any attention to them; this is one benchmark a lot of parents use when trying to differentiate it from a meltdown. On the other hand, meltdown is used to describe the condition where a child loses control so utterly that the behavior only discontinues when they wear themself out or the parent can calm the child down. Usually, a meltdown has no purpose and is beyond a child's control.

Tantrums, whether mild or severe, are indicators that a child is battling with emotions that they can't control, with anger being the leading emotion that causes them to lose their heads and blow up. The child might be overwhelmed by a sense of frustration and injustice when they feel they deserve or need something that is being intentionally withheld from them (a cookie, the video game, something they covet at the toy store) and is overwhelmed by their frustration and sense of injustice.

But then again, anxiety is known to be another big trigger; it causes children to freak out, prevailing over the logic that would allow them to see that their anxiety is out of proportion to the circumstance.

To be more explicit, a temper tantrum ensues when a child is

- frustrated with not getting what they want,
- not able to do what they want, or

- not able to properly communicate.

Typically, a child is likely to stop a tantrum after the following responses:

- Being comforted by a parent or caregiver
- Being given what they want (although not an ideal strategy)
- Being ignored and giving up on their own

Kids who throw temper tantrums are conscious and in control of their engagements and can regulate the level of their tantrums depending on the response they get from a parent or adult. It is possible, however, to employ the use of behavioral strategies to manage tantrums.

Meltdowns, on the other hand, have completely different bases as they are prompted by sensory overload. A child, particularly one on the spectrum, having a meltdown can display a few defining characteristics.

Meltdown symptoms may include the following:

- They typically begin with premeltdown signs referred to as rumblings; these rumblings can be verbal or physical behaviors that signal an imminent meltdown.
- Their meltdowns are preceded by stimming.

- Overstimulation or a detrimental sensory input typically causes their meltdowns.

- Such a meltdown isn't strictly seen in young children alone; they can also happen to teens and adults.

- Their meltdowns occur with or without an audience.

- Their meltdowns linger longer than average tantrums.

Knowing the difference between a tantrum and a meltdown can help with the application of the right strategies to deal with the situation.

f. Meltdowns, Tantrums, and Aggression

For children with ASD, they often display some intensity of aggression when having meltdowns. Aggression refers to ferocious behavior that may consist of thrusting, hitting, throwing objects, striking, and biting. Aggressive behavior can be concentrated toward others or oneself. Studies have shown that both a meltdown and a tantrum can involve aggression.

Accompanying the sensory overload that leads to a meltdown are other reasons why a child with ASD uses aggression. Some children become vicious once an object of comfort is taken away from them, or when they are compelled into doing something they do not want to do. The basic goal of managing aggression is to make sure that the safety of the child and others around them is sacrosanct. Some approaches would involve the removal of the cause of aggression, providing calming toys and activities, and giving the child a safe space where they can calm down.

g. Telling The Difference Between A Sensory Meltdown Vs. Temper Tantrum

i. The intensity of the tantrum. Typically, tantrums have the reputation of reaching high levels of intensity; however, children usually have a level of mindfulness during a tantrum. A tantrum may involve screaming, stamping, or hitting to try and get whatever they desire. In the same way, meltdowns may have the same characteristics, but will likely start at high levels of intensity and continue to escalate.

ii. Length of a meltdown before calming down. Typically, a child throwing a temper tantrum is likely to stop relatively fast if they recognize their actions and behaviors aren't going to get them what they want. Once they are ignored and it fizzles out, then it is likely that it was just a tantrum. Meltdowns will probably make it tougher to calm the child down. The parent might need to take the child away from what is causing the overstimulation in order to begin the process of calming them.

iii. Frequency of the tantrums and their persistence. It is common for children to have tantrums, especially with young kids from ages two to four years. They typically employ such behavior as a way of testing boundaries. Odds are if they don't have their way four times, at least two of those times would end in a tantrum. Meltdowns, however, are not quite as frequent as tantrums.

Regardless of whether or not it's a tantrum or a meltdown, having a strategy on how to handle it is fundamental for parents. Also, recognizing their feelings is one of the most essential things to do, no matter the case. With tantrums, it is important for parents to be resolute in denial. By so doing, the child would ultimately learn that throwing a tantrum isn't an effective way of getting what they want.

On the other hand, meltdowns every so often necessitate temperate care. This is because children have no control over a meltdown; parents have to meet them where they are. Parents must be proactive, quickly swinging into action, from having the child take deep breaths until they calm down to holding them to provide them with a safe space.

h. How Autistic Meltdowns Differ from Ordinary Temper Tantrums

A lot of parents of stereotypical children talk about their child's tantrums as *meltdowns*. The word meltdown comes from the disastrous, dangerous exposure of radioactive material in a nuclear power plant, and few characteristic temper tantrums rise to that level of intensity. Autistic meltdowns, on the other hand, come closer to the innocuous meaning of the term. In addition, autistic meltdowns have particular qualities that make them dissimilar from the average temper tantrum.

i. Qualities of an Autistic Meltdown

An autistic meltdown is bigger, more emotional, longer-lasting, and more difficult to manage compared to the average temper tantrum.

They are also qualitatively different from the average tantrum as they usually come about for different reasons, are amazingly foreseeable, and have diverse outcomes in children with ASD. Precisely, autistic meltdowns are categorized by the following features:

1. Meltdowns are not limited to children

Autistic meltdowns are not restricted to young children on the spectrum. Adolescents, teens, and even adults with ASD may experience meltdowns and, astonishingly, they may come about even among persons with high-functioning forms of autism.

2. Meltdowns are heralded by signs of distress

Autistic meltdowns normally begin with cautionary signals called *rumblings*. Rumblings are noticeable signs of distress that can either be obvious or subtle. Rumblings might begin with a verbal plea to go now or visually obvious signs of distress such as hands over the ears.

3. Meltdowns may involve intense stimming

Rumblings may consist of or progress to *stims,* which are self-stimulatory behaviors, like rocking, pacing, or finger flicking, or other signs of anxiety. Stims are self-calming techniques used by individuals with ASD to aid in regulating anxiety or sensory input. If you see a person with ASD rocking back and forth or pacing, there's a good chance that they are feeling stressed or, alternately, feeling excited.

4. Meltdowns do not have a purpose

Typical tantrums are often cunning in which a child learns that they can get what they want if they cry or scream. By divergence, autistic tantrums are not manipulative: they are genuine cries of distress.

j. How Autistic Symptoms Relate to Meltdowns

If rumblings are cautionary signals of an autistic meltdown, then extreme stimming or another behavioral response that is known as *bolting* can also be seen as emergency signs. Intense stimming, such as high energy rocking, slamming the hand into the forehead, or other obvious signs of agitation, mean a meltdown is imminent. Bolting is a term used to label running away and is more common among very young children or older people with severe ASD. A person with ASD, faced with overpowering sensory input, anxiety, or stress, may simply run from the room to escape the stimulus. While this is a great coping mechanism, bolting can become perilous when the child or adult is uninformed of issues such as oncoming traffic. It's important to be mindful that rumblings are a reaction to stress and sensory overload and not a form of manipulation. While a typical child might throw a tantrum to humiliate or upset a parent and to get their way, children with ASD seldom have the mind-reading tools to calculatedly manipulate another person's emotions.

k. Managing Autistic Meltdowns

When a child or adult with ASD has gotten to the rumbling stage, it may be possible to arbitrate before a meltdown commences. For instance, a child who is astounded by the noise and light at a mall may calm down quickly when taken outside. A child who is nervous about a social situation may be just fine if they are provided with clear direction and support. However, if an intervention doesn't occur or doesn't solve the problem, a meltdown is almost unavoidable.

While some people with ASD simply yell or stamp, many do become overwhelmed by their own emotions. Bolting, hitting, self-abuse, crying, and screaming are all likelihoods. These can be predominantly frightening, and even dangerous when the individual with autism is physically large. When a full meltdown is in progress, it can be tough to manage. Protection, both for the person with ASD and others in the area, is of the utmost importance. The caretaker may be required to move the individual to a quiet room until the meltdown is over. Occasionally, this may require more than one person to avoid injury.

I. The Challenges of Meltdown Mismanagements

While temper tantrums aren't the nastiest behavioral challenges to deal with, recurrent and unpredictable outbursts can undeniably unsettle one's day. Typically, every child goes through phases where temper tantrums are common. But knowing every parent has to encounter and manage them at one time or another doesn't always lessen the humiliation one might experience when their children throw themselves down on the floor kicking and screaming in a public place.

In an attempt to diminish the embarrassment and frustration, parents would try to put a stop to temper tantrums by employing the use of discipline tactics, which in reality make temper tantrums worse. At times, tantrums increase in frequency, and at other times, they become more aggressive in nature. A lot of parents apply punishment strategies, which can be described as the act of exacting a penalty for wrongdoing. Discipline means to teach.

A lot of parenting methods erroneously pay attention to ending a behavior, rather than teaching the child a skill such as how to regulate themselves when they are overwhelmed. If the child is going through a phase where temper tantrums have become regular, here are five parenting mistakes to avoid, as they could make the situation worse.

i. Paying undue attention to a tantrum. It is important to note that attention strengthens behavior, even when the behavior is negative. Saying words like, "*Stop crying, or I'll give you something to cry about!*" or "*Quit acting like a baby,*" will only inspire the child to carry on with their temper tantrum. By the same token, a parent who tries to reason with a child in the middle of a tantrum offers support for the screaming to linger. Saying words like, "*We'll go to the park tomorrow,*" or "*I'm so sorry that you're mad at me for saying you can't have chewing gum. Would you like a cookie instead?*" isn't helpful either. The best strategy to make a tantrum stop is to ignore it. Ward off the eyes, pretending as though you can't hear the screaming, and walking away if you have to will go a long way in quenching the fiery furnace; however, make sure you don't shower your child with any type of attention.

ii. Reassuring the child during a tantrum. In the event that the child cries because they are genuinely unhappy, by all means, comfort them. But if they pound their fists into the floor because they don't want to go to bed, consoling them will only underpin this behavior. Parents should teach their children healthy ways to deal with prickly emotions. When the child uses generally appropriate ways to express feelings, provide reinforcement.

iii. Giving in to the child's demands. Out of sheer extreme anxiety to make the screaming stop, on occasion parents give in to tantrums. Nevertheless each time this is done, by saying, "*OK, fine. Eat another cookie!*" in an effort to get the child to calm down, the parent teaches the child that temper tantrums are a brilliant way to get what they want. Furthermore, the child will learn to throw bigger, longer, and louder tantrums in the future. Even if the parent only gives into temper tantrums once in a great while, the child is bound to learn that tantrums are a powerful way to get what they want.

iv. Repeatedly issuing warning to the child. It is completely wrong to make threats that the parent doesn't plan to follow through with. In addition, repeated warnings have a likelihood of also backfiring. Saying, "*Stop shouting, or you'll have to go for a time-out,*" over and over again, without actually placing the child on a time-out, demonstrates to the child that the parent doesn't mean what they say.

In a situation where snubbing isn't the best course of action, for instance, in the midst of a holiday meal with family, parents can give their child a consequence. The parent can place their child in a separate room for a time-out if required, take away privileges if the child is being disruptive to others, and so on. In addition, it is important to see the tantrum as a way the child chooses to communicate their needs rather than seeing it as undesirable behavior. Parents can then begin to use such tantrums as a form of communication. Tantrums are developmentally fitting and not unusual.

v. Paying off the child. Parents can resort to bribery out of sheer desperation. A humiliated parent who wants their child to get up off the floor may be tempted to say, "*I'll buy you a toy if you promise to get up.*" However, bribing the child will only embolden them to throw more frequent tantrums.

It is important to clarify that rewards are not the same as bribes. Offering upfront rewards can be useful. Simply stating, "*When you stand up and walk, then we can look at getting a treat*" will cue the child to contemplate making a different choice. For instance, before going into a store, say, "*If you use an inside voice and have a good attitude at the store today, I'll give you a sticker.*" However, make it clear that throwing a temper tantrum won't be rewarded.

Chapter 2

A Closer Look at Meltdowns

a. Stages in Meltdowns for Toddlers

A tantrum is one thing all toddlers have in common: messy screaming and flapping limbs, meltdowns to the ground. Some tantrums have very short lifespans, while others seem to linger without an end in sight. Irrespective of the magnitude of the tantrum, tantrums, and meltdowns have a clear pattern or stages. Here are five stages that the tantrums and meltdowns of toddlers typically go through:

i. Denial. Typically, toddler tantrums almost always begin with denial of some sort. Actions such as completely disregarding parental instructions and requests, or a pause with a look of astonishment and disbelief for being denied their way might occur. During this stage, the child hardly hears their parent or guardian, and would happily try to outrun them.

ii. Anger. Once the denial stage passes, which typically comes about when the parent tries to correct the behavior, some grim toddler anger comes about. Verbal attacks are combined with throwing items across the room, shouting, and crying, typically followed by a dead drop to the ground, complete with flapping arms and legs to express just how angry the child is at the parent.

iii. Bargaining. All through the bargaining stage, things get interesting as this is when the child's crafty and creative ways come into play. The child would attempt to bargain for what they want: "*Fine! If I do XYZ, can I have a Popsicle?*" If an unacceptable response is gotten, a new bargain will be thrown out. These interchanges will go on for a few minutes until the child recognizes that bargaining is not going to work.

iv. Depression. Once the depression stage sets in, things start to become pretty annoying. Depression marshals in the fake tears and moments where the parent is made to feel like the worst parent. This is all intended, of course. This is the toddler's last struggle at turning the tables in their favor. Usually, the tears are make-believe and shouldn't be given into.

v. Acceptance. This stage is the most malicious. The toddler will give in, dry the tears, and walk away, leaving the parent to feel like they have won. This is usually far from the truth. This is the stage when the little mastermind moves on to a new genius plan.

b. Stages in Meltdowns for Children with ASD and Other Special Needs

Meltdowns are spontaneous reactions to overwhelming feelings and over-stimulating environments. Meltdowns are not tantrums; the most distinctive difference is that meltdowns are overpowering, while tantrums are voluntary or purposeful and are every so often used to influence a situation to achieve the desired outcome.

Meltdowns by nature may be sensory or behavioral. Sensory sensitivities are the main issue for many people, including those with neurological differences, mental health problems, autism, and other conditions. Sensory processing difficulties are neurological by nature and include difficulties with receiving, processing, and responding to sensory input. It is critical to fathom how these sensory sensitivities may impact a person's behavior and well-being. Time and again with sensory meltdowns, it goes from zero to hundred *fight-or-flight* mode in a matter of seconds and is rarely seen coming. Behavioral meltdowns commonly take place in reaction to overwhelming feelings owing to changes in the environment, increased nervousness, and social interaction or communication complications. These often progressively build.

There are generally three stages to a meltdown; the buildup, the meltdown/shutdown, and recovery.

i. The buildup phase. The buildup stage is also referred to as the anxiety and defensive stage. It typically comprises physical, verbal, and behavioral signs. This is considered to be the best stage for any form of intervention. There are a number of ways to intervene in this stage subject to the type of meltdown: they may include limiting instructions, redirecting, giving a break, introducing a sensory toy, or an engagement in physical activity. It is imperative to remain calm and quiet, employing the use of a safe environment and a cooling-off space, using routine where possible. If the buildup is in connection to sensory sensitivities, then ideally the environment ought to be changed to accommodate the child or remove them from the sensory input. In the event where this may not be possible, the parent might need to bring together tools to help to cope with the situation. These might include for instance the use of headphones to block out noise or the introduction of break cards to use before the environment becomes too overwhelming.

It may look like the following:

- walking in a different pattern

- change body posture (head down, head on desk, tense)

- become much more literal

- change voice tone

- increase in wringing of hands/hypersensitivity to touch/picking at skin

- become slower to respond or increase in vagueness

- distract other students to a great extent

- become more controlling, more rigid, and asking more questions

- give more stock standard answers (I don't know, I forgot, I'm tired)

ii. The meltdown/shutdown phase. This stage entails when behavior becomes fiery and uncontrolled. Here at this stage, it is typically futile to try to reason with the child. This is why the number one priority at this stage should be safety for the child and those around them. It is further recommended that no attempt should be made to teach new skills or redirect emotions, and the parents must not take the behavior personally. Recommended approaches in this stage are centered on shielding, planning, prompting, and preventing any form of harm.

It may look like the following:

- want more control of their environment.

- seek sensory input: repetitive actions, flipping back on chairs, pacing, jumping on a trampoline.

- feel sleepy, stay completely still, and become rigid.

- are unaware of others.

- run away, climb, escape, hide (under the table, outside, etc.)

iii. Recovery phase. The recovery phase is also referred to as the tension reduction phase. Here, actions may differ from person to person; however, everyone involved is probably going to feel emotionally exhausted. It normally consists of either withdrawing or sleeping. The child may feel a lot of guilt, shame, and remorse from these flare-ups. It is important for parents not to bring up or attempt to discuss the incident during recovery; they are expected to wait until both they and the child are well rested and calm.

Once the recovery stage passes, the parent can begin seeking an occasion to discuss the meltdown with the child to reflect on why it happened, and plan to avoid a reoccurrence in the future. The key is to recognize the signs in the buildup stage and intervene than to prevent the meltdown. Meltdowns are nasty experiences for everyone involved and can leave people feeling drained; this is because, in a meltdown, the child is in panic mode and has no control and cognitive function. The child may not be able to answer back and will use typical standard actions, such as swearing, pushing, and hitting to make people move away and leave them alone. A behavior management program will usually be ineffective, and the child would need to finish the meltdown before adults can take any action.

c. The Meltdown Cycle

Children and youth with Asperger's syndrome (AS), high-functioning autism (HFA), and related disabilities do face common problems related to stress and anxiety. Research has shown that this combination is one of the most frequently observed symptoms in these individuals. Anxiety and disquiet in these children are regularly elicited by or results from environmental stress multipliers such as having to face perplexing social circumstances with insufficient social cognizance, social understanding, and social problem-solving abilities, a sense of loss of control, trouble in forecasting outcomes of everyday happenings and behaviors, as well as an innate emotional susceptibility, misunderstanding of social events, and inflexibility in moral judgment that stems from a very tangible sense of social justice violations. The anxiety and disquiet experienced by persons with ASD, AS, HFA, and related disabilities may show forth in the form of withdrawal, dependence on fixations related to limited interests, or unaccommodating cogitation of thoughts, distraction, and hyperactivity. In addition, it might also prompt aggressive behavior, often described as tantrums, rage, and meltdowns.

It is often reported by parents, educators, and mental health professionals that children with AS, ASD, HFA, and related disabilities seem to show aggressive behavior with little or no earlier caution. In truth, such behavior is one part of an ever-increasing three-stage cycle, which would be elaborately discussed below. In addition to the abruptness with which such behaviors are recounted to come about, it is imperative to note that a lot of children and youth with AS, ASD, HFA, and related disabilities stomach the entire cycle oblivious to the fact that they are under stress. That is, while both explicit negative behavior and withdrawal are obvious to their parents, caregivers, or teachers, depending on the child, students with AS, HFA, and related disabilities may not see themselves as being distressed, angry, stressed, or anxious.

Parents, teachers, and caregivers need to work at preventing and decreasing the ruthlessness of behavioral difficulties; people who work and live with children and youth with AS, ASD, HFA, and related disabilities have to appreciate the cycle of tantrums, rage, and meltdowns as well as implement relevant intermediations for each stage that promote self-calming, self-management, and self-awareness.

d. The Cycle of Tantrums, Rage, and Meltdowns

Tantrums, rage, and meltdowns typically come about in three stages, with each of these stages being of variable lengths. These stages include the following:

i. the rumbling stage,

ii. the rage stage, and

iii. the recovery stage.

i. The rumbling stage. The rumbling stage is the first stage of a meltdown. At this stage, the child or youth with AS, ASD, HFA, and related disabilities display explicit behavioral changes that may seem to be inconsequential and unconnected to a resulting meltdown. For instance, the child might lower their voice, tap their foot, clear their throat, tense their muscles, or frown. Some children employ more apparent behaviors, comprising emotional or physical pulling away, or verbally, physically attacking another child or adult.

It is best to inhibit these behaviors from intensifying, and doing so should ensure that the adult who is intervening doesn't become part of a struggle. Interventions during this stage may consist of antiseptic bouncing, proximity control, signal interference, support from routine, just walk, and don't talk, redirecting, and home base.

All of these approaches can be operational in bringing an end to the cycle, and they are priceless in that they can help the child reclaim control with marginal adult support.

1. Antiseptic bouncing.

Antiseptic bouncing has to do with removing the child, in a non-retributive manner, from the environment in which they are experiencing trouble. At school, the child may be sent on a chore. At home, the child may be requested to get an object for a parent in another living space in the house. While doing these undertakings, the child has a chance to redeem their overall sense of calm. Consequently, when the child returns, the problem would have typically shrunk in scale. In addition, the adult is expected to be on hand for support where needed.

2. Proximity control

This approach would entail the teacher moving close to the student who is engaged in rumbling behaviors, instead of just calling the child's attention to behavior. In the same way, parents using proximity control will move near their children. The simple act of standing next to the child can trigger a sense of calm. This approach is particularly interesting, as it can easily be accomplished without the need to interfere with ongoing activity. For instance, the teacher who goes through the classroom during a lesson uses proximity control.

3. Signal interference

Once the parent or teacher notices that the child with AS, HFA, and related disabilities begins to display rumbling behavior, such as clearing their throat or pacing, the parent or teacher uses a nonverbal signal to alert the child into realizing that they are under stress. For instance, in the classroom, the teacher can place themselves in a vintage position where eye contact with the child can be realized, or an agreed-upon signal, such as tapping on a desk, may be used to alert the child. Signal interference may be trailed by an in-seat distress tool, such as squeezing a stress ball, as commended by an occupational therapist. In the home, the parents and the child can come up with a similar signal, say a slight hand movement, which the parents can use when the child is in the rumbling stage. Most times, this approach goes before antiseptic bouncing.

4. Support from routine

Exhibiting a chart or visual schedule of anticipations and events can offer security to children and youth with AS, ASD, HFA, and related disabilities who characteristically require predictability or planning for a change in routine. This simple step can inhibit anxiety and lessen the probability of tantrums, rage, and meltdowns. For instance, the student who is gesturing frustration by tapping their foot may be directed to their schedule to alert them that after they complete the problem, they get to work on a topic of special interest with a peer. In the same way, while running errands, parents can use support from routine by notifying the child in the rumbling stage that their next stop will be at a store the child delights in.

5. Just walk, and don't talk

This approach involves an adult merely walking alongside the student without talking. The adult's silence is key, as a child with AS, ASD, HFA, or related disabilities in the rumbling stage will probably react hauntingly to any adult statement, misconstruing it or rearticulating it beyond recognition. Once this walk commences, the child is allowed to say whatever they wish to without dread of discipline or logical argument. In the in-between period, the adult must maintain their calm, show as little antiphon as possible, and never be argumentative.

6. Redirecting

Redirecting consists of the adult assisting the child in focusing on something other than the task or activity that seems to be upsetting to them. In the event that the source of the behavior is a lack of understanding, the parent or teacher can employ the use of art, cartooning, or stickers to further explain to the child so as to help them get a deeper understanding of the subject. This is usually interesting, engaging, and fun. There are a lot of cartooning interpretative strategies that can be employed to help the child gain clarity and understanding. Occasionally, the child might need to cartoon immediately, while at other times it can be briefly delayed.

7. Home base

A home base is typically described as a place either in school or at home where a child can escape stress. The home base is usually set up to be quiet, with few visual or activity distractions; also, it should contain carefully selected activities that lead the child to calm. In school, resource rooms or counselors' offices may serve as a home base. It is important that the structure of the room supersedes its location. At home, the home base may be the child's room or an isolated area in the house. Irrespective of its location, it is vital for the home base to be seen as a positive environment.

The home base is not necessary a time-out zone or an escape area from classroom tasks or chores. The child can take their class work to their home base, and at home, their chores must be completed after a brief breather in the home base. In addition, the home base may be used at times other than during the rumbling stage. For instance, at the start of the day, the time spent in a home base can be used as a preemptive measure for screening the schedule of the day, acquainting with any changes coming up in the usual routine, making sure that the student's materials are prearranged, or gearing up for particular subjects. At other times, the home base can be used to assist the student in gaining control after a meltdown.

Once an intervention during the rumbling stage has been selected, it is central to know the child, as the wrong practice can worsen rather than decrease a behavior difficulty. For instance, if a student's behavior worsens when verbal information is delivered, an intervention like signal interference, which does not necessitate any talking, may be more suitable to use compared to antiseptic bouncing, which does necessitate talking. Additionally, while interventions at this stage do not take much time to implement, it is worthwhile that adults appreciate the events that trigger the target behaviors so that they can

- be ready to intervene early, or

- teach children and youth tactics to maintain behavioral control during these times.

Another thing to note is that interventions at this stage are purely analgesic. They do not teach the child to make out their frustration or offer a means of handling it.

ii. Rage stage. The child or adolescent is bound to move into the second stage, the rage stage, once the behavior is not diffused during the rumbling stage. At this point, the child is no longer limited and acts spontaneously, emotionally, and occasionally explosively. These behaviors are likely to be expressed via shouting, biting, striking, kicking, destroying property or self-injury, or suppressed via withdrawal. Meltdowns are not focused; once the rage stage comes into being, it most often must run its course.

Throughout this stage, it is important to place prominence on child, peer, and adult safety as well as on the protection of school, home, or personal properties. The finest way to muddle through a meltdown is to get the child to home base, where they can regain self-control. Another thing of immense importance during the rage stage is assisting the person with AS, ASD, HFA, or related disabilities in recovering control and conserving dignity.

To achieve these, adults ought to have developed plans for the following:

a. getting help from educators such as a crisis teacher or principal,

b. removing other children from the area, and

c. providing therapeutic restraint, if necessary.

Once more, no teaching or other interventions can effectually take place during the rage stage.

iii. Recovery stage. Once the rage stage passes and a meltdown runs its full course, a lot of children with AS, ASD, HFA, and related disabilities become quite remorseful and time and again cannot recollect what happened during the rage stage. Some turn out to be brooding, withdrawn, or refute that any unfitting behavior transpired; others become so physically drained that they need to snooze. It is vital to employ interventions at a time when the child can accept them and in a way the child can appreciate and accept them. If this isn't done, the intervention may just recommence the cycle in a more augmented form leading more rapidly to the rage stage. During the recovery stage, children are frequently not prepared to learn. As a result, it is imperative that grown-ups work with them to assist them to once again become a part of their routine, be it at school or home. This is usually quickly achieved when the child is directed to an exceedingly inspiring chore that can effortlessly be accomplished, like an activity related to a special interest.

Children with AS, ASD, HFA, and related disabilities who undergo stressful circumstances may respond by having a tantrum, rage, or meltdown. These behaviors do not occur in isolation or randomly, even though it might seem so at first glance; they are most often linked with motivation or cause. The child who takes part in an unsuitable behavior is making an effort to communicate their needs. For that reason, before deciding on an intervention to be used during the rage cycle or to stop the cycle from arising, it is imperative to fathom the function or role the target behavior plays. The functional assessment delivers a means of pinpointing the conditions under which behaviors in the rage cycle come about and the particular role that the behavior may be serving to the child. This is the first step in developing active interventions. Indeed, without decisive reasons, causes, or conditions under which behavior comes about, it is improbable that an intervention will be operational.

e. Triggers for Meltdowns in Children with Autism Spectrum Disorder

With a lot of children, teens, and adults, especially those on the spectrum experiencing meltdowns, it is important for coping and accommodation tools to be put in place by parents and caregivers. This is because some researchers argue that meltdowns do not necessarily require interventions as much as they require management, as they are a normal reaction to feeling swamped in an overpowering environment that is typically not intended to take into account the needs of neurodiverse people.

Unlike what people may observe, autistic meltdowns are not necessarily behavior problems. They can generally stem from sensory overload, heightened emotions, or difficulty with changes. When the body and mind are incapable of processing what is taking place, kicking, crying, screaming, or shutting down can come about during a meltdown. It's imperative to realize what can trigger a meltdown in the first place, from overstimulation to bumpy social situations. When we better appreciate neurodiverse individuals, then the higher the chances of learning how to better support their needs at the moment.

i. Unexpected routine changes. A lot of people feel most comfortable when they adhere to a routine, so that they know what to expect; this doesn't change the fact, though, that there are some truly impulsive people out there. Things do not always go as intended, which can be unsettling. However, the commotion from a change in routine can appear overblown, and, for some, can lead to a meltdown.

It is important to appreciate the fact that changes in routines can be highly demotivating for individuals with ASD, as they highly depend on structure and routine. This is why dealing with people who suffer from one special need or the other, particularly ASD, requires patience and understanding; don't be upset if they don't go to your long-distance event. It is also important not to get in the way of their routines; this can lead them to a meltdown.

ii. Loud sounds or excessive noise. One common challenge for people on the spectrum is sensory sensitivity; they have a tendency to be overwhelmed when barraged with excessive input from the world around them. Even though they may be sensitive to a variety of things such as sights, noises, smells, tastes, or textures, loud sounds and places with excessive noise can be particularly disorienting. Loud sounds are also frequently found in places that are busy, muddled, and full of people, which can increase overstimulation at the moment.

iii. Overwhelming feeling in a new environment. For individuals with ASD, a new environment can trigger a meltdown in so many ways. A change in routine or intermingling with new people can trigger overpowering anxiety and might necessitate communicating with new people who may not appreciate neurodiversity. It's, therefore, no surprise why a lot of people with ASD claim a new environment can lead to a meltdown. New environments come with a diversity of complications for individuals with ASD; they experience, among other things, misunderstanding, encounter bullying, feel the need to constantly adjust, and so on. These all cause overwhelming emotional roller coasters.

iv. Crowded places. A lot of public spaces are also crowded: the mall, train stations, restaurants, popular tourist destinations, and even theaters. Places, where a lot of people gather, can be extremely overpowering to a lot of the senses and can be the trigger for a meltdown. Even though some individuals with ASD have reported growing out of this displeasure, with their tolerance levels upsurging as they age, a lot still struggle to manage themselves and their emotions whilst in crowded places. This means a lot of people on the spectrum would rather avoid going to the mall, attend weddings, visit clubhouses, and so on.

v. Unattended needs. It's tough for people to be at their best when they are missing out on some of their basic needs, such as food, water, and sleep. It can be disturbing or upsetting when one feels uneasy or tired, and that breeds vulnerability to triggers in the immediate environment, which invariably means meltdowns can be more in the offing to happen during these times.

Meltdowns can be triggered by tiredness, hunger, too much contact, dehydration, and so on. The key to less meltdown is balance; eight hours of sleep, nutritious food with protein, water, and peace.

vi. When people aren't on your level. A lot of neurotypical individuals have no clue as to how to accommodate people with ASD in conversations. Often, conversations end up being mismatched. Also, with jobs that entail lots of social interaction, the distress can easily lead to a meltdown primarily because of the number of interactions that they are bound to have daily. In addition, when the individual with ASD is also hyper-intellectual, which makes them see things "first," they are bound to feel some level of frustration when they see what other people should be seeing, but don't.

vii. Sensory overload. Having superfluous sensitivity to the flora and fauna around them is a trademark of autism; this is why any time their senses get encumbered or overstimulated, they might get inundated and have a meltdown. Overstimulation can include too much light or noise, swarming spaces, or too many activities going on at the same time. In many societies today, however, the creation and use of sensory rooms have been adopted in order to help individuals with ASD cope with sensory overload in public places, such as football stadiums, zoos, and theaters.

viii. Unambiguous or trivial triggers. From time to time, the trigger to a meltdown can be something that seems unimportant and fabulously specific. This could be a slight change in routine, a misused word in a sentence, the texture of one type of vegetable, or one individual pop song on the radio. It is important to note that even though others may not think of little triggers as a big deal, it can be majorly overpowering for individuals with ASD.

ix. When things feel unbridled. It is extremely calming for individuals with ASD to have a specific routine or build a certain amount of predictability into their day. Nevertheless, once things begin to seem out of control or disordered, it can trigger anxiety, overstimulation, or sensory overload, which can ultimately lead to a meltdown. In addition, things can also feel out of control when a sequence of smaller things looks as if they are going wrong all at the same time.

x. Feeling locked in. For individuals with ASD, sustaining comfort within their physical space is essential. However, a meltdown is bound to surface once that space is compromised one way or another. This could imply feeling physically stuck in a small room, ensnared into a conversation, or when someone is perceived to be too far into their personal space. This is an especially true fact that the invasion into their space makes them anxious.

xi. Uncomfortable social interactions. For individuals with ASD, social interactions, when not managed appropriately, can be draining, befuddling and uncomfortable on their own. Due to the peculiarity of ASD, certain kinds of social interaction can also lead straight to a meltdown, especially when there is more than one individual to communicate with all at once. Social discomposure can also seem like being interjected too often or needing to change topics too many times in the same discussion.

People coming from all sides can cause freezing, a breakout of sweat and palpitation, skin irritation, the trigger for tears, and so on. Having to make the brain jump from topic to the topic over and over again can leave the individual shaking, if not worse.

f. Understanding Sensory Implications for Meltdowns

The human body has more than just the five senses to be careful about; it has to contend with all of the sensations from the environment alongside its inert senses. These include the following:

- Sight
- Hearing
- Taste
- Smell

- Touch

- Movement

- Body positions

- Internal body process awareness

For instance, if one's hearing informs them that a scene on a television show is too loud, then they can easily get up and turn the volume down. If the sun is perceived as being too bright, making it hard to see or to pay attention to what is going on around a person; they can put on sunglasses and resume their normal activity.

However, for certain individuals, such as people with sensory processing disorder (SPD), each one can affect someone differently. In the above instances, a person with SPD may have an astounding reaction to something much quieter or less obvious as the noisy TV. Another person with SPD may squint and cover their eyes from the bright sun, but not distinguish the cause or know how to reclaim stability. This may then affect their walk and carrying on with their normal activities, as they may also seemingly shut down, standing in the middle of the sidewalk squeezing their head with their hands. For children often cannot make out, elucidate, or tell how to cope with the incredulous sensory processing system. This explains why an outburst of behavior, the meltdown, comes about.

g. Sensory Thresholds

We all have sensory thresholds, both high and low. A meltdown characteristically comes about when a condition puts a person past their supervisory sensory threshold. Present somewhere in the middle of our sensory threshold is what could be considered the optimal place for self-regulation and normal daily functioning. In addition, our distinctive sensory thresholds vacillate during the day. Once you are tired, your thresholds might be lower, and you might be easily irritable to noises. But if you are well rested and happy, your threshold level would be higher, causing you to enjoy a bit more noise in a social setting.

A person with SPD has thresholds that are higher and lower than normal. A child with a very high threshold might have challenges with poor attention spans, the exhibition of sensory-seeking behaviors, and limited body awareness. On the other hand, someone whose thresholds are very low may have challenges of being overly sensitive, easily overwhelmed, and anxious.

h. Parental Strategies for Helping with Sensory Thresholds

Here are a few techniques for parents to help them cope with their child's meltdowns.

  i. ***Be observant and sensitive to the sensory thresholds of the child.*** It is important for parents to manage a keen interest in how and when their children reach their sensory thresholds. This will help with circumventing the undesirable behavior or and maintaining it if it ever occurs. Here are some common meltdown triggers to look out for:

- Loud noises, such as machinery sounds, traffic, construction, and so on. These are demonstrated by covering the ears, shouting or crying, trembling, being dreadful, hiding behind parents, or clasping to their legs.

- Crowds, owing to being frequently touched and bumped by other people. Some children with SPD categorically abhor being touched, while others are overly grabby or rough when touching other people.

- Bright lights/the sun, as verified by covering of the eyes, grumbling and looking at the ground when walking outside, narrowing the eyes, looking straight at the ground, and having difficulty in sitting still in brightly lit rooms.

- Getting dressed or undressed, owing to the discomfort or even sore sensation of putting on and taking off clothes. Children will every so often fight, get annoyed, cry, lie down and squeal, and kick or hit to avoid being dressed.

- Dining, owing to being fastidious about which textures and temperatures they can eat.

In the case where the child habitually refuses certain categories of foods, such as crunchy, cold, hot, wet, squishy, and so on, then these could be triggers for a meltdown.

ii. ***Recognize how the child responds when approaching their sensory threshold.*** It is important to develop and maintain a keen sense of observation for the child; this will help the parent in deducing the signals that specify that the child is approaching a sensory threshold. From time to time, a meltdown can be elicited by an apparent event, which can easily be recognized.

On occasion, being stunned by choice can cause a child to shut down; shopping is an excellent example. Once confronted with the need and demand to choose, the child may begin to tug at their ears, stare at the ground, and become unresponsive to queries. At such a point, the parent might have missed the chance to notice that the child was approaching sensory overwhelm. At other times, it could be that the child has a buildup of small triggers throughout the day and then blows up at apparently nothing. This often happens to children after school. They use up all their energy in keeping calm through the small triggers at school, but when they reach the safety of home, they completely break down as they cannot hold themselves together anymore.

If the parent perceives that their child experiences meltdowns out of seemingly nowhere, it's very possible that the parent is dealing with a form of escalation of sensory overload. It is important to pay the required devotion to what activities were going on in the child's life for the few hours leading up to their next meltdown. A great way of noticing and catching the trends is by keeping a journal.

iii. ***Identify what behavior to anticipate in the child when they reach their sensory threshold.*** A key question for parents to answer is what does a full-blown meltdown in their kids look like? Some children lie on the ground, screaming and fighting; others cry with wide eyes as if in terror, shaking and sobbing while clinging to you. Still others experience a shutdown, in which they stop talking, cover their ears or eyes, and find a dark corner to hide in, or tuck their knees to their chest and rock. Knowing the reactions of the child during a meltdown can help the parent know the right action to take to resolve it.

iv. ***Pinpoint what works best for relieving the child from a meltdown.*** There are a lot of soothing strategies out there that help kids calm down during a meltdown, but not all work for everyone. It is important for the parent to find out what works best for unwinding their child's meltdown. Once identified, such approaches and strategies should be written down and copies should be given to the child's teachers and other care providers.

Here are a few strategies to try:

- You can hold the child tightly against you and rock slowly.

- You can breathe deeply and slowly while looking into your child's eyes so they can synchronize their breaths with yours.

In addition, parents should formulate a How-Do-You-Feel chart to help their children ascertain how they feel and recognize when a meltdown is building up.

v. ***Give the child a sensory diet.*** A sensory diet is a plan that parents employ in ensuring that their child obtains the sensory-rich activities they seek at steady intervals throughout the day. For children who need more sensory inputs, a typical sensory diet would take in regular periods of play and movement in an area with high levels of sensory stimulation. The child may have four to five movement breaks where they can do jumps on the spot, fitness exercises, enjoy a chewy or crispy snack, carry heavy objects around, or operate a fiddle toy.

For children with low thresholds who are effortlessly overwhelmed, their sensory diet would consist of periods where they can escape to an environment with very low stimulation. And four to six times per day, the child can go to a quiet, low-lit room where they are given a deep-pressure massage with soft music and slow, rhythmic movements for five minutes.

Typically, by taking the time to appreciate some background context for why some children get incredulous by certain situations, parents would be able to help their children reach success in their daily routine. By appreciating sensory thresholds and triggers, parents can be better equipped to diffuse a meltdown before it even begins.

i. Sensory Questions

Characteristically, there are a lot of common questions that parents have about sensory processing and sensory meltdowns. Below are some common sensory queries that parents do ask. On occasion, the feeling of simply knowing one is not alone in their questions and concerns is helpful. So inquiries that frequently arise include the following:

- Parents ask how to better understand their children and help them feel accepted.

- Parents regularly wonder how they can better identify the signs of sensory overload so they can stop it from happening in the first place.

- A lot of times, parents see meltdowns that look to come out of nowhere. You can't appear to figure out what the causes are. Where do you even start?

- Parents every so often feel astounded or hassled with how to react to their child's meltdowns. If this sounds familiar, you might be curious as to whether your child's behavior is sensory or if it is simply insolent behavior.

- Perhaps you might know that your child's meltdowns are sensory related, but nothing you've tried appears to work. You wonder if maybe you're searching for the wrong things or if there is something you've missed.

- Parents marvel if the behavior their child has is a temper tantrum or if it is a response to sensory overload and having a meltdown.

- Parents, time and again, feel like their child is simply trying to get attention, and that it's communicative rather than sensory related.

- Parents often ask about the aggressive behaviors they see from their children. What can cause a child to act out so tangibly with striking, spattering, head banging, biting, scrabbling, and yelling? These actions are physically and emotionally fatiguing for both you and your child.

- Parents ask how they can stay calm at the moment when their child is in the middle of a meltdown. How can they help their child without losing it themselves?

Sometimes, just knowing that others have the same questions is so helpful.

Chapter 3

Managing Meltdowns

a. Self-Regulation

Self-regulation happens to be one of those unusual things that a lot of people are incapable of defining, but everyone notices when it's missing. Self-regulation is the ability to fathom and manage one's behavior and reactions to feelings and things happening around them. It is the way the mind systematizes its working; this is essentially connected to the inflection of emotions. The regulation of emotion is primarily advanced from within interpersonal experiences in a process that institutes self-organizational abilities. Self-regulation comprises being able to

- police reactions to sturdy emotions such as frustration, excitement, anger, and embarrassment,

- calm down after an exciting or upsetting event,

- focus on a task,

- refocus attention on a new task,

- manage impulses, or

- behave in ways that help with getting along with other people.

A person may be unable to self-regulate if

- they stop themself from falling asleep by slapping their face or thrashing their limbs around even when they can barely keep their eyes open.

- they giggle to themself, which spirals into uncontainable laughter or crying for a prolonged period in an unfitting situation, and cannot stop themself.

- they don't realize the difference between feeling hungry or full. They can't distinguish the feeling of wanting to use the bathroom until it's almost too late.

- minor stressors, such as the momentary displacement of a toy, sends them into a panic.

So self-regulation can be broken down in the following order:

i. Self-regulation is a cerebral process that originates from infancy. Typically, each time a parent or caregiver reacts fittingly to a baby's cries, discourses, gestures, eye contact, or other nonverbal forms of communication, the baby is learning cause and effect. The baby learns to adjust their behavior to meet their most basic needs.

ii. Self-regulation is an executive function of the brain. Persons with neurological conditions such as ADHD, ASD, seizure disorders, traumatic brain injury, and even those with no formal diagnosis or who aren't quite neurotypical may find it tough with self-regulation.

iii. Self-regulation is entwined with emotional development. It is normal for one to feel satisfaction when their needs are met and also feel some level of distress when disappointed. Most people learn how to calm themselves during times of anguish. A lot of people also learn when it is fitting to express or suppress different types of emotion.

iv. Self-regulation is entwined with social development. Each time a person intermingles with another person, new social cues are engaged, and behavior subtly becomes accustomed to new people and situations. This implies that it is through others one becomes themself.

b. Why Self-Regulation Is Important

It is important to note that as your child matures, their improved self-regulation abilities would help them in the following ways:

- It will help with their learning at school. This is because self-regulation promotes the child's ability to sit and listen in the classroom.

- It will help with behavior in socially acceptable ways. This is because self-regulation promotes the child's ability to control their emerging impulses.

- It will help with making friends. This is because self-regulation promotes the child's ability to take turns in games and conversation, share toys, and express emotions in appropriate ways.

- It will help with becoming more independent. This is because self-regulation promotes the child's ability to make suitable decisions about behavior and learn how to act in new situations with less guidance from the parent or caregiver.

c. How and When Self-Regulation Develops

Typically, children cultivate self-regulation via warm and responsive relationships. Additionally, they also develop it through watching the adults around them. Self-regulation begins when children are babies. It grows mostly in the toddler and preschool years; nevertheless, it also keeps growing right into adulthood. For instance, babies might resort to sucking their fingers for comfort, or they may look away from their caregivers if they need a break from attention or are getting tired. Tots can wait short periods for food and toys. But they may still snatch toys from other children if it's something they want. And tantrums are bound to break out when tots are overwhelmed by strong emotions.

Youngsters will begin to learn how to play with other children and comprehend what's expected of them. For instance, a youngster may try to speak in a soft voice when watching a movie. School-age children get better at regulating their wants and needs, visualizing other people's viewpoints, and seeing both sides of a circumstance. This implies, for instance, that they might be able to differ from other children without having to descend into arguments. Preteens and teenagers will get better at planning, sticking with tough tasks, behaving in socially fitting ways, and bearing in mind how their behaviors affect other people. For instance, a teenage child may think about their parent's perspective when they are negotiating with the latter about their curfew.

d. Self-Regulation Theory

Self-regulation theory (SRT) frameworks the process and mechanisms involved when one chooses what to think, feel, say, and do. It is predominantly noticeable in the circumstance of making a healthy choice when there is a strong desire to do the opposite.

There are four components involved with the self-regulatory theory:

- standards of anticipated behavior,
- motivation to meet standards,
- monitoring of circumstances and thoughts that go before breaking standards, and
- willpower, allowing one's internal strength to control urges.

These four components act together to regulate one's self-regulatory activity at any given moment. In addition, behavior is determined by one's standards of good behavior, motivation to meet those standards, the degree of conscious awareness of circumstances and actions, and the extent of one's willpower to resist temptations and choose the best path.

d. Self-Regulated Learning

Self-regulated learning (SRL) speaks of the process students take part in when they take responsibility for their learning and apply themselves to academic success.

Typically, such a process transits in three steps:

a) *Planning:* This involves the student planning their tasks, setting goals, outlining strategies to tackle the task, and creating a schedule for the task;

b) *Monitoring:* This involves the student putting their plans into action and closely monitoring their performance and experience with their chosen methods;

c) *Reflection:* This final step involves a reflection on results after the task is complete and the results are in. The student ponders on how well they did and why they performed the way they did.

Once a student takes the initiative and regulates their learning, they gain profound insights into how they learn, what works best for them, and, eventually, they perform better. This improvement spirals from a lot of opportunities to learn during each phase:

a) In the planning phase, the student has an opportunity to work on their self-assessment and learn how to pick the best strategies to succeed.

b) In the monitoring phase, the student gets experience implementing the strategies they chose, making real-time adjustments to their plans as needed.

c) In the reflection phase, the student fuses everything they learned and reflects on their experience, learning what works for them and what should be changed or substituted with a new strategy.

e. The Psychology of Self-Regulation

Experts in the field of self-efficacy and SRT have established that self-regulation is an unceasingly active process in which a person

- observes their behavior, the influences on their behavior, and the consequences of their behavior,

- adjudicates their behavior in relation to their personal standards and wider, more contextual standards, and

- responds to their behavior: this would include what they think and how they feel about their behavior.

It is important to note that self-efficacy plays a major role in the self-regulation process, as it exerts its influence on one's thoughts, feelings, motivations, and actions.

An instance to illustrate the significance of self-efficacy can be seen when two people who are highly motivated to lose weight both actively monitor their food intake and their exercise and also have specific, measurable goals that they have set for themselves. If one of them has high self-efficacy, believing that he can lose weight if he puts in the effort to do so; while the other has low self-efficacy, feeling that there's no way he can hold to his prescribed weight loss plan, it isn't hard to determine who would eventually succeed.

It can be said with reasonable conviction that the man with higher self-efficacy is likely to be more effective, even if both men start with the same standards, motivation, monitoring, and willpower.

f. Self-Regulation Therapy

All forms of therapy, as earlier stated, are focused on self-regulation; they all aim to assist individuals to reach levels of stability in which they are able to efficiently control their own emotions and behaviors and, occasionally, thought patterns.

On the other hand, there is also a form of therapy that is specially intended to nurture SRT and its principles. Self-regulation therapy is based on research findings in neuroscience and biology to help the individual reduce excess activation in the nervous system. Such surplus activation, which includes an off-balance or unsuitable fight-or-flight response, can be caused by an upsetting incident or any life event that is noteworthy or overwhelming.

Self-regulation therapy wishes to assist the individual in correcting this problem by building new pathways in the brain that permit more flexibility and more suitable emotional and behavioral responses to occur. The eventual goal is to turn emotional and behavioral dysregulation into effective self-regulation.

g. Appreciating Ego Depletion

A central SRT concept is that of self-regulatory depletion, also known as ego depletion. This is a state in which a person's willpower and control over self-regulation progressions have been exhausted, and the dynamism set aside for constraining impulses has been spent. It often results in poor decision-making and performance. When an individual has been confronted by many temptations, some of which could be too strong to resist, the person must put forth a correspondingly powerful amount of energy when it comes to controlling their impulses. SRT maintains that individuals have a limited amount of energy for this purpose, and once it's gone, two things tend to happen:

- Inhibitions and behavioral checks are fragile, implying that the individual has less motivation and willpower to abstain from the temptations, and

- The temptations, cravings, or urges are felt much more strongly than when willpower is at a normal, nondepleted level.

This is a fundamental idea in SRT. It elucidates why people struggle to avoid engaging in unacceptable behavior when they are tempted by it over a long period. For instance, it clarifies why a lot of weight-watchers can keep to their strict diet all day, but once dinner's over, they will give in when tempted by dessert. It also elucidates why a married or otherwise devoted partner can reject advances from someone who is not their partner for days or weeks, but might eventually give in and have an affair.

Contemporary neuroscience study backs this idea of self-regulatory depletion. A study used functional neuroimaging to demonstrate that individuals who had depleted their self-regulatory energy experienced lesser amounts of connectivity between the regions of the brain involved in self-control and rewards. This implies that their brains were less cooperative in assisting them to resist temptation after unrelenting self-regulatory activity.

h. The Importance of Self-Regulation

Self-regulation is known to assist in augmenting and upholding a healthy sense of well-being. Generally, there is a lot of evidence that suggests that those who effectively exhibit self-regulation in their everyday behavior revel in greater well-being. Researchers establish that greater self-regulation was positively connected with well-being for both men and women.

The results are similar in studies of young people. A study indicated that teenagers who often take part in self-regulatory behavior report greater well-being than their contemporaries, as well as improved life satisfaction, seeming social support, and good feelings. Conversely, those who bottled up their feelings as a replacement for addressing them head-on experienced lower well-being, as well as greater loneliness, more negative feelings, and worse overall psychological health.

i. Emotional intelligence. One of the many ways in which self-regulation adds value to well-being is via emotional intelligence. Emotional intelligence can be defined as the aptitude to notice emotions, to access and engender emotions so as to help thought, to fathom emotions and emotional knowledge, and to pensively standardize emotions so as to encourage emotional and intellectual growth.

There are five components of emotional intelligence, namely

1. Self-awareness,
2. Self-regulation,
3. Internal motivation,
4. Empathy, and
5. Social skills.

Self-regulation, or the degree to which a person can influence or control their own emotions and impulses, is a dynamic piece of emotional intelligence. This is because it is hard to imagine anyone with high levels of self-awareness, inherent motivation, understanding, and social skills who mysteriously has little to no control over their impulses and is driven by licentious emotion. Emotional intelligence is strongly related to well-being. It should be noted that a healthy understanding and managing of one's emotions and the emotions of others will inevitably lead to making sensible conclusions about our environments, adjusting to them, and pursuing our goals.

ii. Motivation to succeed. Self-regulation is also entangled with motivation. As stated earlier, motivation is one of the fundamental components of self-regulation; it is one dynamic that defines how well we are able to standardize our emotions and behaviors. A person's level of motivation to succeed in their undertakings is directly linked to their performance. Irrespective of the person's best intentions, well-laid plans, and amazing willpower, they will likely fail if the person is not motivated to adjust their behavior and avoid the temptation to slack off or set their goals aside for another day. The more motivated the person is to achieve their goals, the cleverer they would be in striving toward the same. This impacts one's well-being by filling them with a sense of purpose, capability, and self-esteem, particularly when they are able to meet their goals.

iii. Attention-Deficit/Hyperactivity Disorder and Autism. Self-regulation is also an essential topic for people struggling with ADHD or ASD. One of the trademarks of ADHD is a restricted ability to focus and normalize one's attention. Similarly, trouble with emotional self-regulation is deeply associated with ASD. Those on the autism spectrum often have trouble recognizing their emotions; and even if they are able to identify them, they generally have a hard time moderating or regulating their emotions.

Difficulty with self-regulation is well understood as a common symptom of ASD, but effective methods for improving self-regulation in ASD are unfortunately not as well known or regularly implemented as one might wish.

There are more than a few approaches for helping children with ASD in learning how to self-regulate. A lot of these approaches can also be applied to children with ADHD, including the following:

- Revel and build your child's gifts and successes;
- Esteem and listen to your child;
- Endorse your child's apprehensions and emotions;
- Make available clear expectations of behavior, using visual aids if needed;
- Set your child up for success by accepting a one-word answer and providing accommodations;
- Disregard the challenging behavior, such as screaming or biting;
- Substitute tasks, such as doing something fun and then doing something challenging;
- Teach and interrelate at your child's existing level rather than at what level you want them to be;

- Give your child varieties within strict parameters, such as letting them choose what activity to do first;

- Arrange for access to breaks when required; this will give the child an opportunity to avoid bad behavior;

- Encourage the use of safe calm down places as a positive place, not as a place of punishment;

- Set up fortification systems to reward your child for anticipated behavior;

- Permit times and places for your child to do what they want; this must not be an inconvenience or intrusion for anyone else;

- Incentivize flexibility and self-control, verbally and with tangible rewards; and

- Use proactive language to inspire good behavior rather than pointing out bad behavior.

In the long run, helping the child learn to self-regulate more effectively will benefit the parents or caregivers, the child, and everyone they interrelate with and will advance their overall well-being as well.

i. The Art of Mindfulness

Mindfulness can be described as the sentient effort to uphold a moment-to-moment awareness of what's going on, both inside one's head and around them. Mindfulness and self-regulation are a powerful blend for contributing to well-being. Self-regulation necessitates self-awareness and monitoring of one's own emotional state and reactions to stimuli. Being aware of one's thoughts, feelings, and behaviors is the basis of self-regulation, as without it, there would be no skill to reflect or choose a different path.

Teaching mindfulness is a great way to expand one's ability to self-regulate and to improve overall well-being. Mindfulness inspires active awareness of one's thoughts and feelings and helps with conscious decisions about how to behave over merely going along with whatever one's feelings say. There is reliable evidence that mindfulness is an operational tool for teaching self-regulation. Researchers discovered that those in the mindfulness group showed greater attentiveness, a better knack to delay gratification, and more operational inhibitory control than those in the control group. Furthermore, results also submitted that those with the most troubled self-regulation abilities profited the most from the mindfulness intervention, showing that those at the lower end of the self-regulation range are not a lost cause.

j. Executive Function

Mindfulness is a brilliant way of building certain attention abilities, which are part of a larger set of dynamic abilities that let us plan, focus, remember essential things, and multitask more effectively. These abilities are known as executive function skills, and they encompass three crucial types of brain functions:

a) *Working memory:* a person's store of short-term memories or information we recently absorbed.

b) *Mental flexibility:* a person's ability to shift focus from one stimulus to another and apply context-suitable guidelines for attention and behavior.

c) *Self-control:* a person's ability to set priorities, standardize emotions, and resist impulses.

These abilities are not intrinsic; however, they are learned and built over time. They are dynamic skills for circumnavigating the world, and they fund good decision-making skills. When one is able to productively traverse the world and make good choices, they set themself up to meet their goals and enjoy greater well-being.

k. Self-Regulation Test and Assessment

There are two concrete preferences in terms of a self-monitoring scale and self-regulation questionnaire:

- The Preschool Self-Regulation Assessment (PSRA) for children

- The Self-Regulation Questionnaire (SRQ) for adults

The PSRA will work best for young children on self-regulatory strategies. It's labeled as a handy direct assessment of self-regulation in young children founded on a set of organized tasks, containing activities such as the following:

- Balance Beam,
- Pencil Tap,
- Tower Task, and
- Tower Cleanup.

The SRQ is a 63-item valuation measured on a scale from 1 (strongly disagree) to 5 (strongly agree). The items agree to one of seven mechanisms:

- getting relevant information,
- appraising the information and comparing it to norms,
- activating change,
- examining for options,
- framing a plan,
- executing the plan, and
- evaluating the plan's efficiency.

Chapter 4

Managing Meltdowns Continued

a. Early Childhood and Child Development

The expansion of self-regulation begins at a very early age; as soon a child is able to access their working memory, display mental plasticity, and control their behavior, one can get started with helping them develop self-regulation.

b. Teaching and Developing Self-Regulation in Toddlers

Self-regulation in children is a good thing; here are some tips and suggestions on how to go about developing the virtue in toddlers:

- Begin by providing a controlled and predictable daily routine and schedule;

- Modify the environment to eliminate distractions; turn off the TV, dim lights, or provide a soothing object such as a teddy bear or a photo of the child's parent when you perceive the child is becoming upset;

- Role-play with the child to rehearse how to act or what to say in certain situations;

- Frequently teach and talk about feelings; also, review home/classroom rules now and then;

- Permit the child to let off steam by creating a quiet corner with a small tent or pile of pillows;

- Embolden pretend play scenarios among preschoolers;

- Maintain calmness and firmness in your voice and actions even when the child is experiencing a meltdown;

- Expect transitions and provide sufficient caution to the child, or use picture schedules or a timer to notify them of transitions;

- Forward inappropriate words or actions when needed;

- In the classroom or at playgroups, pair the child with limited self-regulatory skills with another who has good self-regulatory skills to serve as a peer model;

- Take a break yourself when required, as children with limited self-regulatory skills can test an adult's patience.

c. Games for Teaching and Developing Self-Regulation in Kindergarten and Preschool Children

The use of games and activities can be employed to assist young children to build their self-regulation skills. Here are a few resources listed below; they are fun and creative ideas for kindergarten and preschool children.

i. Red Light, Green Light. In this game, the children are allowed to move after the *green light* is called, but are to freeze when the *red light* is called. In the case where a child is caught moving during a red light, they're out; it is important to be light-hearted about the game; this will promote fun and effective participation.

ii. Mother, May I? This game is played with one child as the leader. The rest of the children ask: *"Mother, may I take (a certain number of steps, hops, jumps, or leaps to get to the leader)*? The job of the leader is to either approve or disapprove of the action. The first child to touch the leader wins. The element of fun in this game will trigger movements and activity that promote self-regulation.

iii. Freeze Dance. This game involves turning on music and instructing everyone to freeze once the music stops. This is a fun game and will keep the children alert to exercising restrain over their emotions.

iv. Follow My Clap. This game is played with the leader coming up with a clapping pattern. All participating children are to listen and repeat the pattern. This game will promote the ability to pay attention and to mimic others, which are essential skills in self-regulation.

v. Loud or Quiet. In this game, the children are encouraged to perform an action that is either loud or quiet. Let them begin by picking an action, such as stomping their feet. The leader should say "*loud*," which would encourage the children to stomp their feet loudly. This game will promote their sensitivity to sound and the intensity of various emotions.

vi. Simon Says. This game is played by having children perform an action as instructed by the leader, but only on the condition that the leader begins with, "*Simon says...*" For instance, if the leader says, "*Simon says touch your toes*," then all the children are to touch their toes. But if the leader only says, "*Touch your toes*," then no one should touch their toes, because Simon didn't say so. This game will promote keenness to listen to and follow instructions, attention to details, and emotional restraint.

vii. Body Part Mix-Up. This game involves the leader calling out body parts for the children to touch. For instance, the leader might call out "*knees*," inspiring the children to touch their knees. The leader can come up with one rule to begin: for instance, each time the leader says "*head*," the kids should touch their toes instead of their heads. This necessitates that the children stop and think about their actions and not just react. The leader can call out "*knees, head, and elbow.*" The children should then touch their knees, *toes*, and elbow. Continue practicing and adding other rules that change body parts.

viii. Follow the Leader. This game entails the leader performing various actions and the children having to follow those actions exactly. This game promotes their ability to mimic, keep their emotions in check, and focus on various tasks with the aim of accomplishing them to the latter.

ix. Ready, Set, Wiggle. In this game, if the leader calls out, "*Ready…Set…Wiggle,*" all participating kids should wiggle their bodies. If the leader calls out, "*Ready…Set… Watermelon,*" no one should move. If the leader calls out, "*Ready…Set…Wigs,*" no one should move. The game should linger like this. The leader can change the commands to whatever wording they want. The idea is to have the children waiting to move until a certain word is said out loud. This is a very great game for building focus and attention, alongside the ability to restraint one's emotions.

x. Color Moves. In this game, the leader should explain to the children that they will walk around the room. They'll move based on the color of the paper you are holding up. The green paper should indicate a fast walk, the yellow paper should indicate a regular pace, and the blue paper should indicate slow-motion walking. Whenever the leader holds up a red paper, they stop. Try different locomotor skills such as running in place, marching, or jumping.

xi. Classic games. The under-listed are well-known games that can also be used to help your child develop self-regulation. It is recommended that they all be explored by parents and their kids:

- Duck, Duck, Goose

- Hide and Seek

- Freeze Tag

- Musical Chairs

- Mirror, Mirror

d. Self-Regulation in Adolescence

Typically, as a child grows, the parent would perhaps find it difficult to encourage continuing self-regulation skills. On the other hand, teenage years are a dynamic period for further development of these skills, chiefly for the following:

- sticking it out on complex, long-term projects such as applying to college,

- problem-solving skills to achieve goals such as managing work and staying in school,

- deferring gratification to achieve goals such as saving money to buy a car,

- self-monitoring and self-rewarding advancements on goals,

- regulatory behavior founded on future goals and concern for others,

- making decisions with a comprehensive outlook and empathy for oneself and others,

- dealing effectively with frustration and distress,

- seeking help when stress is uncontrollable, or the situation is hazardous.

It is important to support adolescents in developing these essential skills; here are three important steps you can take:

- It is best to teach self-regulation skills by modeling them yourself, presenting opportunities to practice these skills, observing and strengthening their progress, and training them on how, why, and when to use their skills.

- You can provide a warm, safe, and approachable relationship in which your adolescent is comfortable with making mistakes.

- You can also structure the environment to make adolescents' self-regulation easier and more practicable by limiting opportunities for risk-taking behavior, providing constructive discipline, highlighting likely consequences of poor decision-making, and reducing the emotional intensity of conflict situations.

e. The Role of Self-Regulation in Education

Children reach another noteworthy stage of self-regulation development when they start going to school, and self-regulation is tested as school gets more challenging. There are three times when self-regulation can help the learning process:

1. Before starting the learning task, when the student can reflect on the task, set goals, and cultivate a plan to tackle the task,

2. While working on the task, when the student must monitor their performance and see how well their strategies work, and

3. After the task, when the student can reflect on their performance and decide on what worked well, what didn't, and what needs to change.

Generally, teachers are encouraged to do the following things to help students continue to develop self-regulation:

1. Give students a choice in tasks, methods, or study partners as frequently as possible;

2. Give students the occasion to evaluate their work and learn from their errors; and

3. Pay attention to the student's beliefs about their learning abilities and respond with encouragement and support when necessary.

f. Strategies, Exercises, and Lesson Plans for Students in the Classroom

For teachers who are more interested in applying practices and strategies for boosting self-regulation in the classroom, here are a few resources and methods to consider.

i. McGill self-regulation lesson plans. This resource takes in several helpful lesson plans for encouraging self-regulatory skills in students. It includes lessons on the following:

- cognitive emotion regulation,
- acceptance,
- self-blame,
- positive refocusing,
- rumination,
- refocus of planning,
- catastrophe checks,
- positive reappraisal,
- blaming others, and
- putting things into perspective.

ii. College and career competency framework and lessons. The self-regulation lesson plans from the *college and career competency framework* outline nine distinct lessons that can be used to help the students continue to develop their skills. The lessons differ in length from about twenty to forty minutes and can be altered or modified as desired.

The lessons include the following:

- Define Self-Regulation;

- Understand Your Ability to Self-Regulate by Taking the Questionnaire;

- Make a Plan;

- Practice Making a Plan;

- Monitor Your Plan;

- Make Changes;

- Reflect;

- Find Missing Components; and

- Practice Self-Regulation.

g. Self-Regulation in Adults

Even though considerable attention is paid to self-regulation in children and adolescents since that's when those skills are evolving, it's also essential to keep self-regulation in mind for adults. For instance, self-regulation is particularly important in the workplace. It's what keeps a person from yelling at their boss when the latter is getting on the nerves of the former; slapping a coworker who typically gives one a hard time, or from engaging in more nonthreatening but still socially intolerable behaviors such as falling asleep at one's desk or stealing someone's lunch from the office fridge.

People with high self-regulation skills are better able to circumnavigate the workplace, which implies that they are better equipped to get and keep jobs and mostly outclass their less-regulated peers.

To assist you in effectively managing your emotions at work and building them up outside of work as well, here are a few things to try:

- Do mindful breathing exercises;

- Eat healthily, drink lots of water, and limit alcohol consumption;

- Use self-hypnosis to decrease your stress level and remain calm;

- Exercise frequently;

- Sleep seven to eight hours a night;

- Make time for fun outside of work;

- Laugh more often;

- Spend time alone; and

- Manage your work-life balance.

It is possible that these tips come off as very general, but it's a fact that living a generally healthy life is key to dipping your stress and preserving your energy for self-regulation.

h. Cognitive Reappraisal

This approach can be labeled as a sentient effort to change one's thought patterns. This is one of the foremost goals of cognitive-based therapies such as cognitive-behavioral therapy or mindfulness-based cognitive-behavioral therapy. To form cognitive reappraisal skills, one would need to work on changing and reframing one's thoughts when one comes across a challenging circumstance. Embracing a more adaptive perspective to one's circumstance will help in finding a silver lining and in the management of emotion regulation and keeping negative emotions at bay. Cognitive self-regulation has also been established to be positively connected with social operation. It involves the cognitive abilities used to fit in different learning processes, which also helps with support for our personal goals.

i. Skills and Techniques to Improve Self-Regulation in Adults

There are a lot of guidelines you can apply to enrich your self-regulation skills. Begin by reading through these techniques and picking out the ones that resonate with you, then try them out.

1. *Leading and living with integrity*

Being an ideal role model, practicing what you preach, building trusting environments, and living in alliance with your values are essential in your quest to improve self-regulation. Living a life full of dishonesty will do nothing but invite trouble from within and without. The best way to keep the balance is to maintain a noble attitude which comes from leading a life of integrity.

2. *Being open to change*

It is important to challenge yourself to deal with changes in a straightforward and positive way and work tirelessly to improve your ability to acclimatize to different situations while staying positive. Change is indeed inevitable; so living in anticipation of such imminent changes can be both preparatory and therapeutic, as it frees the mind to make the much-needed adjustments. This, in the long run, is good for self-regulation.

3. *Identify your triggers*

One beneficial thing to do to yourself is to cultivate a sense of self-awareness that will aid you in learning what your strengths and weaknesses are and what can trigger you into a difficult mental state. Self-regulation is hinged on a balanced mind, a mind free from unnecessary triggers.

4. *Practicing self-discipline*

Daily investments in self-discipline are extremely rewarding; committing oneself to take initiative and staying dogged in working toward your goals, even when it's the last thing you feel like doing, is an act worth admiring and emulating. Self-discipline will deepen one's hold on their mental and emotional states, thereby improving overall self-regulation.

5. *Reframe negative thoughts*

Negative thoughts are toxic; they can keep you down for a long time. It is important to make a conscious effort into reframing them as they come along. You have to learn to work on your ability to take a step back from your prevailing thoughts and feelings to analyze them and come up with positive alternative thoughts. A close watch over your thoughts can help in arresting toxic thoughts, reframing them for the better, and using them to improve self-regulation.

6. *Keep calm under pressure*

Your mental calm is required for the cultivation and maintenance of self-regulation. This is why it is imperative that you keep your cool by removing yourself from the circumstance for the short term, be it mentally or physically, and using relaxation techniques such as deep breathing;

7. *Consider the consequences*

Every action is yoked with consequences; taking out time to pause and think about the consequences of giving in to unacceptable behavior could trigger a resolution that could help sustain healthier self-regulation. Each carefully thought out step could be made with the future in mind and with the anticipation of a more rewarding consequence;

8. *Believe in yourself*

Furthering your self-efficacy by working on your self-confidence, concentrating on the experiences in your life when you succeeded, and keeping your inaccuracies in perspective are healthy ways of building self-regulation. Deciding on believing in your abilities and surrounding yourself with positive, supportive people is also great for your overall development.

j. Self-Regulation Strategies: Methods for Managing Oneself

Here are a number of strategies that can be adapted for use to self-regulate, both as an individual and as someone in a relationship. The strategies are classified into two groups, namely *the positive or neutral* and *the negative or neutral*. The *positive or neutral* strategies include the following:

- intentionally attend to breathing, relaxing,
- exercise,
- movement,
- mindfulness of body sensations,
- being there to care for one's body, nutrition,
- meditation and prayer,
- self-expression: art, music, dance, writing, and the like,
- caring, nurturing self-talk,
- laughing, telling jokes,
- positive self-talk ("I can," "I'm beautiful" messages), and

- go inside with deliberate nurturing of self.

Relationship: focus on other, negative or neutral, strategies include:

- Look for dialogue and learning;

- Play with others;

- Share humor;

- Develop mutual inquiry; move toward the relationship to learn;

- Desire and move toward collaboration;

- Deliberately honor or celebrate the other; call attention to the other;

- Acknowledge what is said or done and any truth in it;

- Be humorous; and

- Inquire about impact.

k. Emotion Regulation Skills

Emotion regulation skills are fundamental for adults, older children, and teens. They encompass some of the main strategies and skills one can apply to keep emotions under control. Here are four main strategies:

- *Opposite action:* This involves doing the exact reverse of what you feel like doing.

- *Facts checking:* This involves you looking back over past experiences to learn the facts of what transpired, such as the event that caused a reaction, any elucidations or suppositions made, and whether the reaction complemented the intensity of the situation.

- *PLEASE*: This acronym stands for *"treat physical illness/liabilities (PL), eat healthy (E), avoid mood-altering drugs (A), sleep well (S), and exercise (E)."* All of the aforementioned behaviors will aid you in maintaining control over your emotions.

- *Pay attention to positive events*: This entails you keeping the focus on the positive aspects of an experience rather than on the negative, doing your best to engage in a positive activity, and keeping yourself open to the good things.

I. Self-Regulation Chart and Checklist

Even though there are a lot of charts and checklists to work without, there are two handy tools to use with kids, namely *the self-regulation chart and self-regulation checklist.* This self-regulation chart is meant for parents and teachers to fill out and complete, but it is concentrated on the child. It lists out thirty skills linked to emotional regulation and instructs the adult to rate the child's performance in each area on a four-point scale that ranges from *"Almost Always"* to *"Almost Never."*

All of these skills are central to keep in mind, but the skills particular to self-regulation include the following:

- lets others comfort them if upset or disconcerted,
- self-regulates when nervous or troubled,
- self-regulates when the dynamism level is high,
- handles being teased in suitable ways,
- handles being left out of a group very well,
- consents to not being first at a game or activity,
- consents to losing at a game without becoming dismayed or angry,
- says "no" in a satisfactory way to things they do not want to do,
- Accepts being told "no" without becoming dismayed or angry,
- is able to say "*I don't know*", and
- is able to end dialogues appropriately.

The self-regulation chart and checklist can easily be found and downloaded online. Another kind of chart that can assist students with their self-regulation development is *the behavioral self-*

regulation chart. This chart is intended for students to fill out themselves. It comprises four columns with the following questions:

- What happened?
- How did others react?
- What was your reason?
- What else could you have done?

Completing this chart will inspire your child or student to monitor their feelings and behaviors, identify the consequences, evaluate their reactions, and come up with adjustments or spank new strategies to try out next time. A good self-regulation checklist will aid the child or student in assessing their self-monitoring, and keep the goal of self-regulation in mind.

m. Teaching Self-Regulation in the Classroom

*i. **Make rules and expectations abundantly clear.*** This is particularly essential in young children, as explaining what the rules are, what is expected, what is and isn't appropriate, and taking the time to give them regular reminders will ultimately be setting them up to succeed. It is also important to note that the easier the rules are, and the more steadily they are reinforced, the easier it is for the children to do what is expected of them.

*ii. **Employ the use of visual schedules.*** Visual schedules are fantastic for kids who flourish on routine and predictability, as it assists in setting expectations at the start of the day, and for kids who get trapped with schedule changes, it can aid in their preparation ahead of time. By handing out to kids a visual representation of what their day is likely to look like, you endow them by letting them look at the visual schedule and traffic from one activity to the next without the necessity of any form of promptings. *The Easy Daisies Grade 1–7 Classroom Schedule* is a great tool and can be gotten and downloaded online.

ii. ***Concentrate positive reinforcement.*** Reinforcement is a wonderful method that can be employed by either parents or teachers when a child is exhibiting behavioral complications as a result of poor self-regulation. Even though both positive and negative forms of reinforcement can aid in teaching kids self-control, studies lean toward suggesting that positive reinforcement, the deed of rewarding a child when they complete an anticipated behavior as a means of growing the chances that the child would repeat the behavior, is the most effective. Granted, rewarding students for doing what is expected of them isn't continually the desired teaching method; however, something as simple as giving applause in front of the whole class, making a child the *Star of the Day*, or letting a child stand first in line after exhibiting actual self-control can make a huge difference.

iv. ***Teach calming tactics.*** When it comes to teaching self-regulation, kitting kids with fitting calming tactics can make all the difference. Here are some tactics worth exploring:

1. Practice deep breathing

It's common knowledge that taking deep breaths can aid in the restoration of a sense of calm when apprehension resurfaces, and a fantastic way to teach this concept is to encourage kids to blow bubbles when they're feeling apprehensive. Begin by giving each child their bottle of mini bubbles to practice; once they've become skilled at the concept, have them practice blowing bubbles without the wand. This will give them an actual managing tactic they can use when big emotions hover to take over during the school day and beyond.

2. Use rewards

It is no secret that children are enthused by rewards, and a sticker chart can be very effective for children who scuffle with self-regulation. Granted, making unconnected sticker charts for each student would be quite labor-intensive. However, making a classroom sticker chart whereby every student can earn stickers for the whole class by exhibiting emotionally suitable reactions (this can include sitting quietly during circle time, lining up at the door when the school bell goes off, helping to clean up after an activity, and so on), and organizing a special treat for the entire class to enjoy once a certain number of stickers has been gotten can get everyone thrilled.

3. Make a calm down box

Another way to assist children to learn self-regulation is to equip the classroom with a calm down box. Fiddle toys, squeeze balls, and chewing gum are all fantastic classroom-appropriate ideas that can aid in reducing the feelings of anxiety and in restoring a sense of calm.

4. Cultivate a "calm down corner"

It is important to have a chosen area within the classroom where students can take a break when they feel incredulous; this is a great way to assist them in keeping emotions in check. This may necessitate a bit of encouraging from the teacher at first, such as, *"I notice you're feeling a little frustrated. Why don't you go to the Calm Down Corner for a few minutes?"* However, teaching the kids how to be aware of their emotions and arming them with tactics to calm down before things get any worse is particularly valuable.

5. Make transitions slowly

Transitions tend to be fast and furious, especially in a classroom setting. A typical class can experience up to eighteen transitions in ONE day, which can be tough for any child, particularly those for whom self-regulation is quite tough to handle. Finding ways to slow down transitions is key for children who struggle; this can be done with individualized education programs. This may imply that some kids take part in fewer activities throughout the day; nonetheless if it helps them deal with their environment and reduces negative reactions; then it is absolutely an approach to think through.

n. The Zones of Self-Regulation

The *Zones of Regulation* is a mental behavior-based syllabus intended to assist children in learning how to normalize their emotions self-sufficiently. This is typically done by teaching them how to recognize their feelings and how their behavior influences those around them. The program teaches kids how to recognize when they are in diverse emotional states referred to as *zones*, which are epitomized by different colors. The *Zones of Regulation* uses activities to arm children with the tools they need to control their actions and stay in one zone, or perhaps move from one zone to another; this allows them to gain amplified control and problem-solving abilities. The *Zones of Regulation* isn't the only tool out there that one can use to help teach children self-control. There are lots of other strategies that can be used to set a child up for success.

o. The Colors in the Zones of Regulation Program

The *red zone* is a much-amplified state of alertness with intense emotions and is characteristically seen as the child being out of control. *Red zone* behaviors may include the following:

- anger
- rage
- out of control
- mad
- physical reactions
- terror
- extreme feelings

- feeling ready to explode
- devastation

Activities aimed at counteracting the *red zone* may include the following:

- Movement
- Heavy work
- Running, walking
- Deep breaths
- Listening to music
- Talking to someone
- Activities listed under the other zones

The *yellow zone* is the child reaching an amplified state of alertness and eminent emotions are characteristically seen as heading toward the *red zone*; however, the child is seen as still having some measure of control. Examples of *yellow zone* behaviors include:

- anxiety
- undulating
- silliness

- fretfulness
- vexed
- frustration
- excitement

Activities aimed at counteracting the yellow zone may include the following:

- Do stretching exercises
- Perform Yoga asanas
- Relish nature
- Drink a glass of water
- Listen to music
- Write in a journal
- Activities listed under the other zones

The *green zone* is the prime level of vigilance and is characteristically seen, as the child is good to go and prepared for learning and social interactions. Instances of the *green zone* behaviors include the following:

- positive reactions

- calm
- ready to go
- happy
- attentive
- contented

Green zone activities may include the following:

- Write in a journal
- List out accomplishments
- Help someone
- Reach out to a friend
- Activities listed under the other zones

The *blue zone* is a low level of vigilance characteristically seen as the child running leisurely. Instances of *blue zone* reactions include the following:

- sick
- bored
- tired

- sad

Blue zone activities may include the following:

- Talk to someone

- Rest

- Build a puzzle

- Read a book

- Color or draw

- Think about positive mindset strategies

- Activities listed under the other zones

p. Zones of Regulation Activities

One of the significant things about the *Zones of Regulation* is the point that there is no one *right* zone to be in. in a way; it can be all right to be in the *red zone* or the *yellow zone* as we all have vacillations of dispositions and behaviors. The most important part for us, however, is to propose approaches to assist children in understanding and identifying their feelings and emotions. It's essential for children to fathom how their reactions impact others, principally when they are not able to keep a lid on their emotional or behavioral reactions.

All the aforementioned *Zones of Regulation* activities can be swapped and used, as they are able to help the child transit from one zone to another. It is important to note that each child will respond differently in each zones strategy: some strategies might work wonders in others, while others might need to be tweaked or even substituted with another.

1. Zones pocket play for emotions and coping approaches folders

In this zones activity, children can make the tools they need to work on self-regulation.

- o Begin by having the children fold file folders to make a pocket on the bottom.
- o They can trim off the edges once done.
- o Hot glue can be used to turn the large pocket into four sections, which are red, yellow, green, and blue.
- o Instruct them to color and label the sections based on zones.
- o You can have the children label craft sticks with either emotions or coping strategies and insert them into the correct pockets.

These *zones pocket play for emotions and coping approaches folders* can be employed for use in the home or classroom.

2. Zone check-in tubes

- o You can get the children to paint or wrap colored tape around paper towel tubes in accordance with the zone colors.

- If painting, encourage them to wait to dry.
- Follow up with each child writing emotional words or even drawing emotional facial expressions onto the matching tube color.
- You can place a hairband onto the tube to roll up and down as required to perform check-ins with children throughout the day.

3. Zone check-in frames

- You can create hot glue colored craft sticks according to zone colors (red, yellow, green, and blue), use them in creating a square frame, and then have the children write the zone title on one side and zone emotion words on the other side.
- Alternatively, you can have the child write zone emotion words on one side and coping strategies on the other side.
- Place a clothespin onto the frame to clip as required to implement check-ins with children throughout the day.

This tool can also be used to teach and appraise while learning the program zones.

4. Zone grab bag game

- You can get the children to create an emotion identification grab bag game. This can be done in a number of ways:

- Get the kids to draw emotional expressions as faces on corresponding color dot stickers, and have them placed on bottle caps (for younger children).

- You can have the kids simply draw emotional facial expressions on bottle caps directly with a black marker (for older children).

- Have the children draw emotional facial expressions on plastic spoons with matching colored markers (for younger children).

- Draw emotional facial expressions on plastic spoons with a black marker (for older children).

- Once these are crafted, throw only the caps or only the spoons into a grab bag or simply throw them all into one bag.

- When children grab a cap or spoon from the bag, they choose which matching color they belong to find the correct emotion and zone.

5. *Zones of regulation craft*

This activity uses a lion and lamb craft for self-regulation to pinpoint emotions and talk about *lamb* emotions and reactions and *lion* emotions and reactions.

6. *Coping skills toolbox*

- Begin by identifying coping approaches that work for each child, as this can make all the difference in having a set of workable regulation approaches when the need presents itself.

- o Write them out on slips of paper, add them to a flipbook, make them into coping skills Popsicle sticks, or add them to a coping strategies bulletin board.

- o Kids can go through numerous calming and alerting activities and use them to self-regulate.

7. *Zone of regulation chart*

- o Begin by using a file folder or sliding a paper into a page protector to create a *Zones of Regulation* chart using movement activities in the classroom.

- o Kids can mark off their zone and pick from a coping mechanism to help them get to a zone in which they can learn and pay attention.

q. Keep a Self-Reflection Journal

Using a printed journal such as the *Self-Reflection Journal* or *the Impulse Control Journal* can aid children in identifying more about themselves and becoming more self-aware while pondering on their day and week. You can encourage them to write down their actions, emotions, and responses and then look back at what worked and what didn't work. By employing a written journal, kids can define good and poor selections that they've made and then write out tools that they can try next time. Journaling is referred to as a conversation tool employed when speaking about what works and what doesn't work for a child with a diversity of needs.

The Impulse Control Journal is even more elaborate than the *Self-Reflection Journal*, as it works on the compulsions that impact behavioral or emotional regulation and the actions that follow. This tool is operational in assisting children and teens in identifying emotions, reactions, responses, and learning approaches to change their regulation through self-awareness. Kids can select strategies freely and see progress by working through the *Impulse Control Journal* pages.

r. Identify Emotions through Play

One of the fundamental steps of self-regulation is the aptitude to identify emotions. Social-emotional learning starts with naming emotions and matching emotion names to faces and body language. When children pinpoint emotions, they can begin to grow empathy for others but also become more self-aware of their own emotions, the things that sway those feelings, and how they react. Some ways to identify emotions through play include the following:

- Use play to pinpoint emotions through various pretend-to-play activities.

- Use pictures or video modeling to assist kids in identifying emotions and labeling the terms.

- Act out emotions with toys, and name the emotions that the toys are demonstrating.

s. Explore Self-regulation Skills

When children walk around exploring self-regulation skills by trying out with sensory input, they can detect the rapports that their body feels when they are open to that sensory input. If done all through a calm period, when the child is at high alert and focus, they are able to completely experience the input without interruptions. Children can then create a zones toolbox using the self-regulation skills that work for them.

Here are a few self-regulation skill explorations to try with kids:

- You can experiment with a variety of sensory foods and ask the child to pinpoint how their mouth feels with each food.
    - Does the food taste salty, sweet, chewy, crunchy, or sour?
    - How does their mouth feel after trying each food?
    - Are they awake, sleepy, happy, calm, or alert?

Ask the child to put a name to each food. Mark these down on a chart, and use this as a regulation tool.

You can experiment with different kinds of movements using *Sensory Diet Cards*. Kids can try the sensory activity and pinpoint how their body feels. Mark it down, and add those calming or alerting activities to their regulation toolbox.

Chapter 5

Managing Tantrums

a. Anatomy of a Temper Tantrum

Temper tantrums often come about, as young children are not armed to express frustration in other ways. Even their limited languages can make them feel exasperated to the point of throwing a fit. Maybe the child wants a toy, but don't have the clout to purchase the toy. Maybe they want to stay at a friend's house, but their parents say that it's time to go. These events can turn into tantrums, particularly when children are put in circumstances that can spur strong emotions. The behavior characteristically diminishes once the child gets enough attention or have their desires met.

b. How to Manage and Prevent a Temper Tantrum

Managing tantrums can be very complicated, exhausting, and fretful; however, one does not need to possess any academic degrees in psychology or biology to be able to successfully bring and keep it under control. Trying out countless approaches to managing the outbursts, and doing so at every opportunity is a good way to get going, which would eventually land you on the right approaches as time passes. Finally, discovering techniques that work for your child, even on playdates, can be exhilarating. Below are a few techniques that you can apply; it is however important to note that not all techniques will be effective for every child. It is best to try a handful, with an eye out for the ones that best fit your child:

Rule One: It's not about you.

It is important to understand that the experimentation and implementation of these techniques are primarily about helping your child. The goal behind managing a child's meltdowns is to lessen their frequency, duration, and ruthlessness by modeling respect and empathy.

Rule Two: Define the motivation for the tantrums.

Each episode of this undesirable behavior can be grouped into three basic types, which are

- temper tantrums,
- sensory meltdowns, and
- panic attacks.

Each of these types has different inherent causes and would necessitate different interventions.

c. Causes of Temper Tantrums

Temper tantrums are initiated by feelings of helplessness and loss of control. No one, not even a dominant adult, can control everything at all periods; however, it is a hard lesson for a small person with no decisive power over their environment. It has been observed by quite a few researchers that temper tantrums typically occur most frequently during the month before a child makes a momentous developmental leap of some kind, such as learning to walk, or speak in sentences, or dress themselves, or read sight words. A number of children are able to turn their tears on and off at will during tantrums, which can be annoying for parents. A lot of pediatricians do recommend leaving a child alone in a safe place, like a crib or playpen during a tantrum, then coming back to talk to the child about it afterward. However, some have found this method to be counterproductive or even dangerous for the child, as it might weaken the child's trust in the parent, which can further escalate and prolong the tantrums. In addition, the tantrums may also become more frequent.

i. An emotional sneeze. Tantrums are very much like emotional sneezes; they are natural responses meant to expel whatever can be considered a foreign matter. It is, therefore, best to witness and validate the child's feelings while keeping the child safe from harming themself. It is recommended that during a tantrum, the child should be moved to a quiet place, not as a punishment, but for confidentiality and self-respect, with the parent remaining close at all times.

ii. Temper tantrums in public. When your child throws a tantrum in a public place, the typical thing to do is to go back to your car or a quiet side of a building outdoors. If it happens at a playdate, it would imply going back home or asking your friends to come back on another day. However, the key to not startling away your friends or strangers in this situation is self-confidence. At home, the finest place for a tantrum is in a bedroom where the child can strike and stomp on a mattress.

The fear here is whether allowing such exhibition of needless behavior would be tantamount to spoiling the child and teaching them to manipulate—far from it. This is because tantrums are neither naughtiness nor uncharacteristic or requiring correction. If a child is expressly punished for exhibiting temper tantrums, they will eventually learn not to express their feelings but to suppress them instead, which is not healthy for their body or mind. This is why parental responses and reactions are advised to be gentle, yet firm.

iii. Write a story. One way you can help the child out is by encouraging them to write about their tantrums. Their emotional stories can be in the style of social stories, written in the first person using simple language. Each story can begin with the problem and end with the resolve. Together, you all can read and reread that story now and then. The child can keep adding more stories to the collection over the years, as they recall the details of more temper tantrums. These stories can later become part of their autobiography, and they can begin to develop empathy for others through those stories. What's more, the child's temper tantrums will hold a deeper meaning to them and may be critical to their progress in language and social skills.

Rule Three: Breathe

It is important to take out time to calm yourself and live up to your emotional needs. Then reschedule.

d. Sensory Integration Tools for Meltdown Management

Sensory meltdowns are typically linked with ASD and other neurological conditions; however, anyone can become overstimulated in certain environments. Like typical tantrums, sensory meltdowns can be brought under control by exhibiting respect and responsiveness and searching for the origin of the meltdown. On the other hand, different kinds of meltdowns need different kinds of management. Research has shown that sensory meltdowns are the easiest kind to inhibit, but only if a person is armed with the right tools at the right instant.

e. The Role of Self-Regulation

It is a well-known fact that both sensory-seeking and sensory-avoidant persons may spiral into a sensory meltdown as a result of difficulties associated with self-regulation. Weakened processing produces weakened output; complications with emotion regulation and self-calming only aggravate the dysfunctional patterns of information processing, making it less probable that the child would be able to correct the problem by themselves. The upside of all these is that a person can learn how to work through and divert sensory meltdowns with loving support.

f. Sensory Integration Toolkits

A sensory meltdown typically takes place when there is some sort of discordance in at least one of the senses, namely

- smell,

- taste,

- sight, whether lighting or coloring,

- sound, either too much noise or an exasperating kind of noise,

- touch, whether texture or temperature, and

- balance or spatial awareness.

When a meltdown begins, it is essential to take out a child from the unbearable sensory input and to replace that with calming sensory input.

g. When Away from Home

It is recommended that parents carry along with them a portable sensory toolkit for circumstances that may prove nerve-wracking. Subject to the child's unique sensitivities, some items in the kit may include the following:

1. Sunglasses

2. Hand lotion or lip balm

3. A stuffed animal

4. Chewy snacks, such as beef jerky or granola bar

5. Baseball cap or wide-brimmed hat

6. Squeeze ball or *Koosh* ball

7. Ice-cold water bottle with a sports cap for sucking

8. A piece of soft fabric such as velour for rubbing on hands

9. Soundproof headphones

10. Change of clothes

11. Carrier for a child under forty pounds such as Ergo or Beco carriers ergonomically designed to distribute the child's weight to parent's hips

h. When at Home

When at home, if your child experiences a meltdown, here are a few things that can help you manage the situation effectively:

1. Mini trampoline

2. A stuffed animal

3. Chamomile tea

4. Body sock

5. Deep hugs or sandwiching between two body pillows

6. Heating pad: it is very calming when placed on the back of the neck

7. Silly putty, playdough, or play slime

8. Back rub or massage seat

9. A favorite video or song: this works best for undersensitive children

10. Ear, hand, or foot massage

11. Handheld massage ball

12. Weighted blanket or vest

13. Wooden foot massager

14. Giant exercise ball for sitting and bouncing

15. Rocking chair, swing, slide, or climbing structure

16. Lavender essential oil or chamomile essential oil: you can apply a single drop behind the ears

17. Massage jet for the bathtub

i. When at Playdates and in School

A lot of these items can be combined into playdates or even a school classroom to preclude meltdowns. A caregiver needs to explain to the child during a calm moment why these tools are required and how to request them. Diverse tools will work on different days, as the sensory needs change. Over a period, the child will learn how to use the tools when required. A child is successfully self-regulating when they are able to pick the correct tools for sensory integration. As sensory integration grows, the child will be able to stomach increased sensory input.

Chapter 6

Managing Panic Attacks

a. How to Manage and Prevent a Panic Attack

A panic attack is an abrupt occurrence of intense fear that elicits severe physical reactions when there is no real threat or obvious cause. Panic attacks can be very fearsome. When panic attacks occur, it could be mistaken for a total loss of control, an imminent heart attack, or even feelings of dying, especially if the casualty is a young child.

It can be hurtful to watch one's child scuffle with panic attacks. The parent might feel helpless and not know where to turn, or what to do to help their child. Nevertheless, it's imperative to know that you're not alone, and there are steps you can take to help your child. A lot of people, including children, experience just one or two panic attacks in their lifetimes, and the problem goes away, maybe when a traumatic situation ends. However, if a person has persistent, unanticipated panic attacks and spends extensive periods in endless fear of another attack, then they may have a condition referred to as *panic disorder*. Even though panic attacks themselves aren't deadly, they can be terrifying and can considerably affect one's quality of life.

b. Panic Attack Symptoms

Characteristically, panic attacks arise abruptly, without caution. They can strike at any time when a child is on the playground, when the teen is out shopping at the mall, or when the adult is driving their car or in the middle of a business meeting. This occurrence may be occasional, or it may be frequent. Panic attacks have a lot of variants, but indications typically peak within minutes. What's more, after a panic attack subsides, the victim might feel fatigued and worn out. Panic attacks usually comprise some of these signs or symptoms:

- sense of imminent doom or danger
- fear of loss of control or demise
- fast, pounding heart rate
- perspiring
- quaking or shaking
- shortness of breath or tightness in your throat
- shudders
- hot flashes
- unsettled stomach
- intestinal cramping
- chest pain

- headache

- dizziness, lightheadedness, or faintness

- numbness or tingling sensation

- the feeling of unreality or detachment

One of the most awful things about panic attacks is a strong fear that another one is coming. A victim might fear having panic attacks so much that they avoid certain circumstances where such attacks may occur.

c. When to See a Doctor

If a child experiences panic attack symptoms, the parent can seek medical help as soon as possible. Panic attacks, while extremely uncomfortable, are not hazardous. However, panic attacks are hard to manage on your own, and they may get worse if no interventions are administered. Panic attack symptoms can also bear a resemblance to symptoms of other serious health complications, such as a heart attack; so it's vital to get the victim assessed by a primary care provider if you aren't sure what's causing the symptoms.

d. Causes of Panic Attack

The causes of panic attacks or panic disorders are unknown; however, the following factors may play a role:

- genetics

- major stress

- temperament that is more sensitive to stress or predisposed to negative emotions

- certain changes in the way parts of your brain function

Panic attacks may come on abruptly and without caution at first, but over time, they're typically prompted by certain circumstances. Some studies advocate that the body's natural fight-or-flight reaction to danger is involved in panic attacks. For instance, if a rabid dog came after a person, their body would react impulsively, with their heart rate and breathing speeding up as their body prepares for a deadly situation. A lot of the same responses take place in a panic attack. But it's unknown why a panic attack takes place when there's no apparent danger present.

e. Risk Factors

Symptoms of panic disorder often begin in the late teens or early adulthood and affect more women than men. Factors that may grow the risk of developing panic attacks or panic disorder include the following:

- family history of panic attacks or panic disorder

- major life stress, such as the demise or serious illness of a loved one

- a harrowing event, such as sexual assault or a serious accident

- major changes in life, such as a divorce or the addition of a baby

- smoking or excessive caffeine intake

- history of childhood physical or sexual abuse

f. Complications

Left unattended, panic attacks and panic disorder can affect almost every area of life. One may be so afraid of having more panic attacks that they would live in a constant state of fear, ruining their quality of life.

Complications that panic attacks may cause or be linked to include the following:

- advancements of particular phobias, such as fear of driving, or leaving one's home

- recurrent medical care for health worries and other medical conditions

- circumvention of social circumstances

- complications at work or school

- downheartedness, anxiety disorders, and other psychiatric disorders

- amplified risk of suicide or suicidal thoughts

- alcohol or other substance misuses
- financial difficulties

For certain individuals, panic disorder may comprise *agoraphobia*, shunning places, or circumstances that cause anxiety, as they may fear being unable to escape or get help if they have a panic attack. Or they may become dependent on others to be with them if they must leave their homes.

g. Prevention

There are no definite ways to prevent panic attacks or panic disorder. However, these recommendations may help.

- Get treatment for panic attacks as soon as possible to aid in stopping them from getting any worse or becoming more frequent.

- Stick with the proposed treatment plan to aid in the prevention of a relapse or the worsening of panic attack symptoms.

- Engage in regular physical activity, which may play a role in guarding against anxiety.

h. Ways to Stop a Panic Attack

Here are a few strategies to employ in managing an ongoing panic:

i. Employ deep breathing. Even though hyperventilating is a symptom of panic attacks, which can increase fear, deep breathing, on the other hand, can reduce symptoms of panic during an attack. If the breathing can be effectively controlled, the victim is less likely to experience hyperventilating that can make other symptoms worse, including the panic attack itself. The victim should concentrate on taking deep breaths in and out through their mouth, feeling the air slowly fill their chest and belly and then slowly leave them again. They can breathe in for a count of four, hold for a second, and then breathe out for a count of four.

ii. Be aware of the imminent panic attack. By recognizing and acknowledging that a panic attack is imminent, instead of a heart attack, the victim can remind themselves that this is temporary and that it will pass. In addition, such recognition and acknowledgment take away the fear that the victim might be dying or that impending doom is approaching—both symptoms of panic attacks. This can allow the victim to focus on other techniques to reduce their symptoms.

iii. Close eyes. Some panic attacks come from prompts that overwhelm the victim. If they are in a fast-paced environment with a lot of stimuli, this can feed their panic attack. Encouraging them to shut their eyes will drastically reduce the stimuli and the panic attack, as this action would block out any extra stimuli and make it easier to focus on their breathing.

iv. Practice mindfulness. Being mindful can help ground the victim in the reality of what's around them. Since panic attacks can affect a feeling of disinterestedness or separation from reality, mindfulness can combat the panic attack as it approaches or when it eventually comes about. So it is important to ask the victim to focus on the physical sensations that they are familiar with, such as digging their feet into the ground or feeling the texture of their jeans on their hands. These particular sensations ground the victim firmly in reality and give them something objective to focus on.

v. Find a focus object. Certain people find it supportive to find a single object to focus all of their attention on during a panic attack. Pick one object in clear sight and intentionally note everything about it as much as possible. For instance, the victim may notice how the hand on the clock jerks when it ticks, and that it's slightly lopsided. They can describe the patterns, color, shapes, and size of the object to themselves while focusing all of their energy on this object; in no time, the panic symptoms will eventually subside.

vi. Employ muscle relaxation techniques. Just like deep breathing, muscle relaxation techniques can help stop a victim's panic attack in its tracks by controlling their body's responses as much as possible. They can willfully relax one muscle at a time, starting with something simple, such as the fingers in their hand, and move their way up through the rest of their body. Muscle relaxation techniques are known to be most effective when they are practiced beforehand.

vii. Picture a happy place. It is often rewarding when a victim of a panic attack decides to focus on a vivid imagination of their happy place. It could be a sunny beach with gently rolling waves or a cabin in the mountains. By placing themselves there in the middle of their happy place and doing their best to focus on the details as much as possible, they usher in calm and relaxation. It is important for this happy place to be quiet, calm, and relaxing, not busy, crowded, and noisy streets, no matter how much you love the cities in real life.

viii. Engage in light exercise. Endorphins keep the blood pumping in precisely the right way. Exercises can aid in the flooding of the body with endorphins, which can improve our mood. Because the victim is stressed, let them select light exercises that are gentle on the body, such as walking or swimming. The only exemption to this is if the victim is hyperventilating or struggling to breathe. It is best to do what is necessary to catch their breath first before embarking on any exercise.

ix. Keep lavender on hand. Lavender possesses properties that are known for being soothing and stress relieving. It can aid in relaxing the body. If one knows that they are prone to panic attacks, it is important for them to keep some lavender essential oil on hand and put some on their forearms when they experience a panic attack, breathing in the scent. The victim can also try drinking lavender or chamomile tea, as both plants are relaxing and soothing. However, lavender should not be pooled with benzodiazepines as this combination can cause extreme drowsiness.

x. Repeat a mantra internally. Repeating a mantra can breed relaxation and reassurances; in addition, they can give the victim something to grasp onto during a panic attack. Mantras can be simple, "*This too shall pass,*" or any that speaks to one personally; the victim should repeat it on loop in their head until they feel the panic attack receding.

xi. Take benzodiazepines. Benzodiazepines may help treat panic attacks if one is taken as soon as one feels an attack coming on. Even though other methods to the treatment of panic may be better, the field of psychiatry has recognized that there is a handful of individuals who will neither respond fully nor at all in some cases, to the other methods listed above and as such, will be reliant on pharmacological methodologies to therapy. These methods may often include benzodiazepines, some of which carry Food and Drug Administration approval for the treatment of this condition, such as alprazolam (Xanax). Since benzodiazepines are a prescription medication, the victim will probably need a panic disorder diagnosis in order to have the medication on hand. Please note that this medication can be highly addictive, with the body adjusting to it over time. Therefore it should only be used parsimoniously and in cases of extreme need.

i. Cognitive-Behavioral Therapy

Cognitive-behavioral therapy (CBT) is a kind of psychotherapeutic treatment that supports individuals in learning how to isolate and change negative or troubling thought patterns that have a negative influence on their behavior and emotions. Cognitive-behavioral therapy concentrates on changing the reflex negative thoughts that can add to and worsen emotional problems, depression, and anxiety. These impulsive negative thoughts have a harmful influence on moods. Through CBT, these thoughts are recognized, defied, and swapped with more unbiased, realistic thoughts.

j. Types of Cognitive-Behavioral Therapy

Cognitive-Behavioral Therapy incorporates a variety of techniques and methods that tackle thoughts, emotions, and behaviors. These can go from controlled psychotherapies to self-help resources. There are a number of explicit types of therapeutic approaches that involve CBT. Which type of CBT fits best for your child will be determined by the nature of the child's precise complications, the results of prior remedies, the child's unique background, their penchants, their unique strengths, and weaknesses.

i. Behavior therapy. After traditional Freudian therapies reached their crescendo, behavior therapy became the foundation of a contemporary methodology to therapy. Behavior therapy (BT) was the first of the accurately scientifically proven therapies. The behavioral science of learning, which is how we learn to respond emotionally, behaviorally, and cognitively, is still the foundation of all modern CBTs.

Today, BT is still practiced by world-renowned specialists, as its rudimentary interventions such as exposure or exposure response prevention, which is a kind of desensitization, may still be the most prevailing treatment for anxiety disorders. In addition, BT continues to prove its efficiency as a treatment for major depression.

Other instances of behavioral interventions comprise behavioral activation, social skills training, and communication training. The most recent research trials continue to validate just how vital behavioral change and activation are to changing all other aspects of our responses, such as thinking and emotions.

ii. Cognitive therapy. This specific type of CBT is currently being practiced as the primary form of therapy all over the world. Cognitive therapy stresses directly altering how we think. By altering how we think, we can alter our emotional and behavioral responses. Cognitive therapy accentuates interventions such as evidence-based thinking, premises testing our thoughts, activity scheduling, and forecasting.

It is the most scientifically established therapy for depression and anxiety disorders; scientifically verified controlled research trials have revealed that its efficiency is time and again comparable to medication therapy. In addition, CT has also gone on to accrue hundreds of confirmed actual results for anxiety disorders, personality disorders, eating disorders, phobias, marital discord, ADHD, AS, and the like. Ever since CT became the most proven and endorsed type of therapy, a lot of psychotherapists now claim to know how to do CT; unfortunately, however, very few are credentialed or trained to do so.

iii. Cognitive-behavioral therapy. Cognitive behavior therapy is fundamentally an integration of both cognitive and behavioral therapies. It is one of the most highly acclaimed and scientifically proven combinations of the modern therapies mentioned above. It is a broad term used to talk about a broad, nonspecific amalgamation of BT and cognitive type therapies. When used lightly, the term CBT is occasionally used interchangeably, even though mistakenly, with the term CT; and while the two may share resemblances, in principle CT speaks of a more specific brand of CBT.

Technically, CT accentuates a more thought-focused set of interventions. Cognitive behavior therapy, when delivered by a truly trained and experienced CBT provider, successfully combines the best that modern science can offer in employing all of the interventions developed within traditional and third-generation CBTs. Everyone now claims to do CBT; however, few have been educated, trained, overseen, and experienced in providing the real deal.

iv. *Acceptance and commitment therapy.* Acceptance and commitment therapy (ACT), alongside other *third-generation* CBTs, are still very absorbed in some of the main principles of CBT: the rank of behavior, empirically founded theory and treatments, the significance of dealing with our inner experience, and so on. All CBTs, including ACT, share a keen liking for the effects of thoughts on a person's life; however, ACT more entirely explores the role of approval in our emotional and cognitive enigmas. It stresses bureaucratic knowledge as a way of learning what illogically happens when we try too hard to control our thoughts or inner emotions. In its place, it presents and explores mindfulness exercises as another way to reexperience acceptance of our inner states. This is highlighted as a lot of emotional disorders can be aggravated by efforts at over control, overcompensation, compulsiveness, emotional avoidance, and other forms of rigid misguided handling. Acceptance and commitment therapy integrates mindfulness exercises, a present orientation, value exploration and commitment to gradual action toward our values, a nonliteral involvement of our thoughts, and an expanded definition and experience of our self.

Scientists have generated alternative ideas and methods for reexperiencing or reacting to our inner lives, reevaluating the purpose of our lives, and therefore redirecting attention and action in our lives.

v. Dialectical behavior therapy. This is one of the leading CBT treatments to integrate the scientific principles of traditional CBT, the result of which has courageously glowed the way into new third-generation CBT territory. This therapy was originally developed to treat the most complex and intractable types of syndromes, such as personality disorders, impulsive, and suicidal symptoms (borderline personality disorder in particular). Dialectical behavior therapy (DBT) has displayed results, where other treatments failed. It has since been useful in a variety of personality difficulties and other complex and chronic cases. It is based on a dialectical philosophy that dares us to face and make our peace with the complex and opposite truths, often intrinsic in many situations.

The most rudimentary of these inconsistencies being between accepting ourselves or changing ourselves. It is a skill-based approach, which inspires balancing the best of our emotional and objective selves. Its core skill is mindfulness, learning a nonjudgmental, present-centered intentional awareness, and applying this mindful awareness to life through the other major DBT skills: emotion regulation, distress tolerance, and interpersonal skills. Dialectical behavior therapy has been efficaciously used to a wide diversity of problems where emotional dysregulation and destructive impulsivity have inhibited living. Dialectical behavior therapy treatment has been applied not only to personality problems but substance abuse, trichotillomania, eating disorders, explosive anger, depression, and anxiety.

vi. Functional analytic psychotherapy. *Functional analytic* psychotherapy (FAP) is a relational form of therapy that can be employed in the treatment of a wide range of complications such as anxiety disorders. Additionally, it can also be used to improve our ability to approach challenging life circumstances with bravery and care. FAP challenges both therapist and client to use the time in the session to raise heedful awareness for our behavior, noticing how and where it works and where it doesn't.

Functional analytic psychotherapy goes on to practice courage by opening up to our emotions and finally discovering a sympathetic way of encouraging and maintaining working purposeful behavior beyond the session and into our daily lives. The three elements of practicing FAP include mindful awareness, courage, and loving acceptance (ACL); these are at the very heart of this third-generation form of BT.

vii. Compassion informed psychotherapy. In recent times, experimental and scientific information about how the brain works are shedding new light on how evolution has helped our brain to develop some very distinctive social and emotional capabilities. Therapies such as compassion focused therapy (CFT) and mindful self-compassion (MSC) therapy, are taking advantage of this new science by incorporating it into relational therapies. These compassion therapies practice and develop these very distinctive forms of social-emotional acumen, in and out of session, to treat anxiety and depression, while improving our day-to-day lives.

viii. Mindfulness-based cognitive therapy. Mindfulness-based cognitive therapy (MBCT) is one of the first extended cognitive therapy practices to officially incorporate mindfulness into responding to thoughts. It is founded on mindfulness-type treatments such as mindfulness-based stress reduction, which has had remarkable scientific outcomes with chronic pain, hypertension, gastrointestinal disorders, and other medical disorders. Scientists have presented good results with MBCT for treating intermittent chronic depression. Mindfulness-based cognitive therapy underscores changing not only the content of our thoughts but our responses to our thoughts. This therapy focuses on distancing ourselves mindfully from our thoughts by applying a greater awareness of how we evaluate our thoughts, and how this propensity then adds to our having secondary emotions, for instance, when we get depressed about having depressed thoughts. Mindfulness and a considerate perspective aids in breaking this rancorous cycle common to many pensive type processes and teaches us to continually refocus on making choices to advance day-to-day, minute-to-minute lives.

ix. Integrative couples behavior therapy. Integrative couples behavior therapy (ICBT) has incorporated the best scientific principles of couple's behavior change and conflict resolution, with the extremely essential acceptance of our partner's feelings and traits. Through communication tools such as empathic listening, a better appreciation of how we love the very physiognomies we may also hate in our partners, we may learn to modify our hopes and assumptions about our partners.

This is pooled with committed efforts at conflict resolution: problem definition, brainstorming, hypothesis testing, revisiting the results of the experiment, and integrating what had been learned. Communication skills are thought out, as are pleasure planning and positive tracking.

While each type of CBT takes an altered approach, all work to address the causal thought patterns that add to psychological distress.

k. What to Expect During a Cognitive-Behavioral Therapy Session

Typically, your first session will aid the therapist in grasping the challenge you or your child is dealing with and what you hope to achieve with CBT. Once this is established, the therapist will then frame a plan to achieve a specific goal. Goals should be

- **S**pecific
- **M**easurable
- **A**chievable
- **R**ealistic
- **T**ime-limited

Contingent on your situation and your SMART goals, the therapist might endorse individual, family, or group therapy. Sessions in general last about an hour and take place once a week, even though this can vary based on individual needs and convenience. An important part of the process is homework; so you or your child would be asked to fill out worksheets, a journal, or perform certain tasks between sessions.

Some of the essential tools needed for achieving any level of success are open communication and feeling comfortable with your therapist. If you don't feel comfortable with your therapist, try to find another therapist that you can connect with and open up to more easily. Look for a therapist who is trained in CBT and who has experience treating your specific problem. Also, do check to make sure they're appropriately certified and licensed. You may want to talk to your doctor or other health-care providers for recommendations.

Practitioners may include

- psychiatrists,
- psychologists,
- psychiatric nurse practitioners,
- social workers,
- marriage and family therapists, and

- other professionals with mental health training.

Most times, CBT takes a few weeks to a few months for results to begin to show; so don't be in a rush.

I. Techniques Used With Cognitive-Behavioral Therapy

The main principle behind CBT is that thought patterns have an impact on emotions, which, in turn, can affect behaviors. For example, CBT emphasizes how negative thoughts can lead to negative feelings and actions. However, if one can reframe their thoughts in a more positive way, it can lead to more positive feelings and helpful behaviors. Therapists are trained to teach their clients how to make modifications that can be implemented right away. These are skills that can continue to be used for the rest of one's life.

Contingent on the issue being dealt with and the goals in focus, there are a number of ways to approach CBT.

Whatever approach your therapist takes, it will include

- isolating specific problems or issues in your daily life,
- becoming mindful of infertile thought patterns and how they can sway your life,
- isolating negative thinking and reforming it in a way that alters how you feel, and
- learning new behaviors and putting them into practice.

After speaking with you or your child and learning more about the issue you want help with, your therapist will choose the best CBT strategies to use. Some of the techniques that are most often used with CBT include the following strategies:

i. Cognitive restructuring or reframing. This comprises taking a firm look at negative thought patterns. Maybe you have a habit of overgeneralizing, assuming the worst will happen or placing far too much meaning on minor details. Thinking this way can have an impact on what you do and can even become a self-fulfilling prophecy. Your therapist may ask about your thought process in particular circumstances, so that you can isolate negative patterns. Once you're cognizant of them, you can learn how to reframe those thoughts, so that they're more positive and productive.

ii. Guided discovery. In guided discovery, the therapist will familiarize themselves with your perspective. Then they'll ask questions aimed at challenging your principles and widen your thinking. You might be asked to give substantiation that funds your suppositions, as well as substantiation that does not. In the process, you'll learn to see things from other viewpoints, principally ones that you may not have reflected on before. This can help you pick a more useful path.

iii. Exposure therapy. Exposure therapy can be employed when confronting fears and phobias. The therapist will gradually render you to the things that incite fear or disquiet while giving you guidance on how to deal with them at the moment. This is typically done in small increments. In the end, exposure can make you feel less susceptible and more confident of your coping abilities.

iv. Journaling and thought records. Journaling is a time-esteemed way of getting in touch with your thoughts. Your therapist may ask you to list out negative thoughts that arose to you between sessions, as well as positive thoughts you can pick instead. Another writing exercise is keeping track of the new thoughts and new behaviors you put into practice since the last session. Putting it down in a journal can help you see how far you've come.

v. Activity scheduling and behavior activation. One thing that is guaranteed to help is putting back on the calendar activities that you delisted or put off due to fear or anxiety. Once the burden of decision is gone, you may be more likely to follow through. Activity planning can aid in establishing good habits and in providing sufficient opportunities to put what you've learned into practice.

vi. Behavioral experiments. Behavioral experiments are characteristically used for anxiety disorders that comprise catastrophic thinking. Before getting on a task that ordinarily makes you anxious, you'll be asked to foretell what may likely happen. Later, you'll talk about whether or not the prediction came true. Over time, you may begin to see that the foretold catastrophe is not very likely to happen. Also, it is probable that you would begin with lower anxiety tasks and build up from there.

vii. Relaxation and stress reduction techniques. In CBT, you may be taught some broad-minded relaxation techniques, such as the following:

- deep breathing exercises
- muscle relaxation
- imagery

You'll learn practical skills to assist you in lowering stress and increasing your sense of control. This can be useful in dealing with phobias, social anxieties, and other stressors.

viii. Role-playing. Role-playing can support you in working through different behaviors in hypothetically challenging circumstances. Playing out likely scenarios can reduce fear and can be used for the following:

- cultivating problem-solving skills,
- achieving awareness and confidence in certain situations,
- practicing social skills,
- assertiveness training, and
- refining communication skills.

ix. Successive approximation. This comprises taking up tasks that appear overwhelming and breaking them into smaller, more attainable steps. Each successive step builds upon the previous steps so that you gain confidence as you go, bit by bit.

m. What Cognitive-Behavioral Therapy Can Help With

Cognitive-behavioral therapy can be employed as a short-term intervention to assist individuals in learning to focus on present thoughts and beliefs. It is also used in the treatment of a wide variety of conditions such as

- Addiction
- Anger issues
- Anxiety
- Bipolar disorder
- Depression
- Eating disorders
- Panic attacks
- Personality disorders
- Phobias

In addition to mental health conditions, CBT has been shown to assist people in coping with the following:

- Chronic pain or serious illnesses

- Divorce, or break-ups

- Grief or loss

- Insomnia

- Low self-esteem

- Relationship problems

- Stress management

n. Benefits

The fundamental idea behind CBT is that thoughts and feelings play a central role in behavior. For instance, an individual who spends plenty of time thinking about plane crashes, runway accidents, and other air disasters is likely to avoid air travel as a result. The aim of CBT is to teach people that while they cannot entirely control every facet of the world around them, they can take control of how they deduce and deal with things in their environment. Cognitive-behavioral therapy is often known for the following key benefits:

- It lets you participate in improved thinking patterns by becoming cognizant of the negative and often impractical thoughts that inhibit your feelings and moods.

- It is an effective short-term intervention option; for instance, improvements can be realized in five to twenty sessions.

- It has been seen to be effective for a wide range of maladaptive behaviors.

- It is frequently more reasonably priced compared to some other types of therapy.

- It has been seen to be effective online as well as face to face.

- It can be employed for those who don't need psychotropic medication.

One of the utmost remunerations of CBT is that it aids clients in developing coping skills that can be useful both now and in the future.

o. Effectiveness

The cognitive approach addresses how thoughts and feelings affect behaviors, unlike other earlier behavior therapies that focused almost completely on associations, reinforcements, and punishments to modify behavior. Today, CBT is one of the most widely studied forms of intervention and has been proven to be operational in the treatment of a variety of mental conditions, including anxiety, depression, eating disorders, insomnia, obsessive-compulsive disorder, panic disorder, posttraumatic stress disorder (PTSD), and substance use disorder.

- Cognitive-behavioral therapy is the leading evidence-based cure for eating disorders.

- Cognitive-behavioral therapy has been confirmed as useful in those with insomnia as well as those who have overall medical conditions that inhibit sleep, including those afflicted with pain or mood disorders such as depression.

- Cognitive-behavioral therapy has been systematically verified to be effective in treating indications of depression and anxiety in children and adolescents.

- A 2018 study established that CBT aided in the improvement of symptoms in people with anxiety and anxiety-related disorders, including obsessive-compulsive disorder and PTSD.

- Cognitive-behavioral therapy has a high level of pragmatic support for the cure of substance use disorders, helping improve self-control, avoid triggers, and develop coping mechanisms for daily stressors.

Cognitive-behavioral therapy is one of the most researched types of therapy, in part due to the fact that the treatment is fixated on highly specific goals, and results can be measured comparatively easily.

p. Things to Consider

There are a number of challenges that individuals may encounter during the course of CBT, some of which are the following:

i. Difficulty in changing. At first, some patients submit that while they know that certain thoughts are not balanced or healthy, simply becoming conscious of them does not make it easy to alter them.

ii. The rigid structure of cognitive-behavioral therapy. Cognitive-behavioral therapy doesn't lean toward a focus on causal cataleptic resistances to change as much as other approaches, such as *psychoanalytic psychotherapy*. It is regularly best suited for clients who are more at ease with a structured and focused approach in which the therapist frequently takes an instructional role.

iii. The willingness to change. For CBT to be operational, the patient must be prepared and eager to spend time and effort examining their thoughts and feelings. Such self-analysis and homework can be demanding, but it is a great way to learn more about how inner states impact outer behavior.

v. ***Gradual progress*** *in* cognitive-behavioral therapy. In most cases, CBT is an ongoing process that helps an individual in taking incremental steps toward a behavior change. For instance, someone with social anxiety might begin by merely imagining anxiety-provoking social circumstances. Subsequently, they might begin to practice conversations with friends, family, and acquaintances. By increasingly working toward a larger objective, the process seems less overwhelming and the goals easier to achieve.

q. Things to Keep in Mind

Cognitive-behavioral therapy can be exceptionally supportive. However, if you decide to try it, there are a few things to keep in mind:

i. It's not a cure. Therapy can help improve issues you're going through, but it will not inevitably eradicate them. Mental health issues and emotional distress could continue, even after therapy ends. The goal of CBT is to assist you in developing the skills needed to deal with problems on your own, in the instant when they come up. Some individuals may see the approach as training to provide their therapy.

ii. Results take time. Cognitive-behavioral therapy typically lasts between five and twenty weeks, with one session each week. In your first few sessions, you and your therapist may probably talk about how long therapy might last. That being said, it'll take some time before results will start trickling in. If you don't feel better after a few sessions, you might be tempted to think therapy isn't working. But give it time, and keep doing your homework and practicing your skills between sessions. Undoing patterns set in motion over time is major work, and so go easy on yourself.

iii. It isn't always fun. Therapy can test you ardently. It often aids you in getting better over time, but the process can be tough. You'll need to talk about things that might be throbbing or upsetting. Don't worry if you cry during a session, such actions and events are all expected as you travel the road to success.

iv. It's just one of many options. While CBT can be useful for a lot of people, it doesn't work for everyone. If you don't see any results after a few sessions, don't feel disheartened. Check in with your therapist. A good therapist can assist you in recognizing when one approach isn't working. They can usually recommend other approaches that might help more.

r. How to Get Started

Cognitive-behavioral therapy can be an operational intervention choice for a variety of psychological issues. If you feel that you or someone you love might profit from this form of therapy, consider the following steps:

- Consult with your physician, and check out the directory of certified therapists offered by the National Association of Cognitive-Behavioral Therapists to locate a licensed professional in your area.

- Consider your personal preferences, as well as whether face-to-face or online therapy will work best for you.

- Contact your health insurance to see if they cover CBT, and if so, how many sessions they cover per year.

- Expect your initial experience to be similar to a doctor's appointment, as well as filling out paperwork such as Health Insurance Portability and Accountability Act forms, insurance information, medical history, current medications, a questionnaire about your symptoms, and a therapist-patient service agreement. If you're participating in online therapy, you'll likely fill out these forms online.

- Be prepared to answer questions about what brought you to therapy, your symptoms, and your history, including your childhood, education, career, relationships (family, romantic, and friends), and current living situation.

Cognitive-behavioral therapy is an approach that is widely recommended by physicians. It discourses the thought processes behind the emotions and teaches adaptability in the appearance of adversity. Here is a four-step approach to CBT:

i. Calm the nervous system.

- Practice your favorite calming method until it comes naturally to you. Then the method will be at your disposal in your moment of need.

- Learn how to relax using breathing practices such as *Diaphragmatic Breathing* or *Yoga breathing* exercises.

- Employ sensory integration to soothe the nervous system.

- Get a lot of aerobic exercises. Work your way up to an intensive thirty-minute or forty-five-minute workout four times per week.

- Employ massage therapy.

- Take turns with your child to envisage the worst anxiety-provoking circumstances. Let the imaginary circumstance become as silly as possible.

- Keep a journal about fear and anxiety.

- Visualization of positive imagery works best with children over the age of three or adults.

- Meditation, prayer, chanting, and singing are all well-documented methods for calming the nervous system.

ii. Create an ingenious plan.

- Be familiar with other points of view, and look at the problem from a different standpoint. The casual exploration of other perspectives can prove to be beneficial in overcoming phobias.

- Be honest with yourself about your abilities and limitations.

- Drive yourself to try new proficiencies to gain new insights, even if it is terrifying.

- Develop family ceremonies to get rid of anxiety. A ritual is any practice that is intentionally and regularly performed, such as mealtimes, birthdays, or Saturday morning routines. The whole family will benefit.

iii. Persist in the face of obstacles and failure. The prevalent obstacle in overcoming fretfulness is that it usually gets worse before it gets better. The creative imaginations will triumph if we persist.

iv. Evaluate and adjust the plan. It is important to keep track of emotions during the treatment process. This will help in determining if something is not working so that it can be changed. The idea behind treating panic attacks is to uphold the victim's quality of life and ability to function in everyday life.

s. Agoraphobia

Agoraphobia is a type of anxiety disorder in which the victim fears and avoids places or situations that might cause them to panic and make them feel stuck, helpless, or embarrassed. The victim fears an actual or anticipated situation, such as using public transportation, being in open or enclosed spaces, standing in line, or being in a crowd. The anxiety is triggered by fear that there might be no laid-back way to escape or get help if the anxiety increases. Most people who have agoraphobia develop it after having one or more panic attacks, making them worry about having another episode and avoid the places where it may happen again.

People with agoraphobia often have a tough time feeling safe in any public place, particularly where crowds gather. They may feel that they need a buddy, such as a relative or friend, to go with them to public places. The fear can be so devastating that they may feel unable to leave their home. Agoraphobia treatment can be perplexing, as it typically implies defying one's fears. But with psychotherapy and medications, the victim can escape the trap of agoraphobia and live a more enjoyable life.

t. Symptoms of Agoraphobia

Typical agoraphobia symptoms include fear of the following:

- leaving home alone
- crowds or waiting inline
- enclosed spaces, such as movie theaters, elevators, or small stores
- open spaces, such as parking lots, bridges, or malls
- using public transportation, such as a bus, plane, or train

These circumstances do cause anxiety, as the victim fears that they won't be able to escape or find help if they begin to feel be frightened or have other incapacitating or embarrassing symptoms. In addition,

- Fear or anxiety almost always stems from exposure to the circumstance.
- The fear or anxiety is out of proportion to the actual threat of the situation.
- They avoid the circumstances, need a companion to go with them, or endure the circumstance but are extremely distressed.

- They experience significant distress or problems with social situations, work, or other areas in their life because of the fear, anxiety, or avoidance.

- Their phobia and avoidance usually lasts six months or longer.

u. Panic Disorder and Agoraphobia

Certain individuals have a panic disorder in addition to agoraphobia. Panic disorder is a type of anxiety disorder in which a person experiences sudden attacks of great fear that reach a peak within a few minutes and trigger intense physical symptoms. One who doesn't know might assume that the person has totally lost control, is having a heart attack, or even failing.

Fear of another panic attack can lead to avoiding similar circumstances or the place where it occurred in an attempt to prevent future panic attacks. Signs and symptoms of a panic attack can include the following:

- rapid heart rate

- trouble breathing or a feeling of choking

- chest pain or pressure

- lightheadedness or dizziness

- feeling shaky, numb, or tingling

- excessive sweating

- sudden flushing or chills

- upset stomach or diarrhea

- feeling a loss of control

- fear of dying

v. When to See a Doctor

Agoraphobia can brutally limit one's ability to meet people, work, attend important events and even manage the details of daily life, such as running errands. It is important to see a physician if the symptoms of agoraphobia are seen in increasing measure.

w. Causes of Agoraphobia

Below are some causes of agoraphobia:

- biology: this includes health conditions and genetics,

- temperament,

- environmental stress, and

- learning experiences.

All the above can play huge roles in the development of agoraphobia.

x. Risk Factors

Agoraphobia can begin in childhood, but usually starts in the late teen or early adult years, typically before age thirty-five; however, older adults can also develop it. Women are diagnosed with agoraphobia more often than men are. Risk factors for agoraphobia include the following:

- having panic disorder or other phobias,

- responding to panic attacks with excessive fear and avoidance,

- experiencing stressful life events, such as abuse, the death of a parent, or being attacked,

- having an anxious or nervous temperament, and

- having a blood relative with agoraphobia.

y. Complications

Agoraphobia can significantly bind one's life's activities. If a person suffers from severe agoraphobia, they may not even be able to leave their home. Without treatment, certain people become housebound for years. They may not be able to visit with family and friends, go to school or work, run errands, or take part in other normal daily activities. They may become dependent on others for help. Agoraphobia can also lead to or be associated with the following:

- Depression,

- Alcohol or drug abuse, and

- Other mental health disorders, including other anxiety disorders or personality disorders.

z. Prevention

There's no sure way to prevent agoraphobia. Nevertheless, anxiety tends to increase the more one avoids circumstances that they fear. If one begins to have mild fears about going to places that are safe, it is advisable to try to practice going to those places over and over again before their fear becomes devastating. If this is too hard to do by oneself, the help of a family member or friend can be sought to go with or seek professional help.

If you experience anxiety going to places or have panic attacks, get treatment as soon as possible. Get help early to keep symptoms from getting worse. Anxiety, like many other mental health conditions, can be harder to treat if you wait.

aa. Prevention Summary

The fact remains that preventing a meltdown is by far easier than trying to stop one after it kicks in.

i. Preventing temper tantrums. To prevent temper tantrums, offer some control over trivial matters to the child. For instance, if your child usually resists putting on pajamas at bedtime, you can let them choose their pajamas; this will elicit much-needed cooperation. You can also prevent tantrums by stating expectations and family rules at the beginning of the day. This is because everyone needs limits.

Since temper tantrums are an essential part of emotional development, writing tailored emotional stories about tantrums and reading those stories often can be another preventive method.

ii. Preventing sensory meltdowns. Sensory meltdowns can be prevented by crafting a sensory-friendly environment at home, and carrying a sensory toolkit whenever you are away from home. This will help a sensitive individual develop lenience for new kinds of sensory input and learn how to self-regulate.

iii. Preventing panic attacks. Panic attacks can be prevented by pinpointing the triggers for anxiety as well as supportive lifestyle changes, such as habitual exercise or creative expression: visual or performing arts, woodwork or metalwork, jewelry making, music, writing poetry or fiction. Creativity is a remedy for the inflexibility in personal habits that often accompanies anxiety. Calming routines, such as diaphragmatic breathing, prayer, guided imagery, or exercise, can be built into everyday life so that they are accessible when a panic attack is looming. Review and adapt your strategy as necessary.

Behavior is communication, and communication is a two-way street. Being approachable to all communication attempts is the only way to maintain a constant flow of feedback. Therefore, communication is a type of prevention. Prevention is the key to meltdown management.

Chapter 7

Sensory-Friendly Planning

a. Tips for Planning a Sensory-Friendly Birthday Party

Planning a party for your child can be hectic, especially if the child is highly sensitive. Admittedly, a lot of parents have given up on such plans, as their attempts in the past left them with nothing but bitter experiences, or they simply cannot cope with the many hurdles that they would need to overcome for the party to be a success.

Here is how to plan a Sensory-Friendly Birthday Party:

i. Use a theme your child likes. Adopt a theme that your child would be fond of. The theme at most sensory-friendly parties is "*have much fun without having a meltdown.*" Planning a theme-based party can be fun and very comforting to focus on the birthday person's special interest, such as Legos, trains, or horses.

ii. Have your guests in mind. For families dealing with a highly sensitive child, holding a party strictly being attended by only members of the family is something that can be done. However, bringing in other friends and loved ones can help in many ways. First, the child gets to mingle around familiar faces, people who are understanding and who shower the child with a lot of love and respect the child's limitations. The child gets to receive gifts from guests and is exposed to just the right amount of people, enough to help sharpen their intermingling needs. It is important for all of the guests to be people who will be very understanding and compassionate when the birthday person needs to take a break, even if the birthday person needs to stop the party abruptly and send everyone home.

iii. Find a familiar location. A birthday party is not a good time to acquaint with a new environment to the birthday person. For this reason, the home is typically the best location for a sensory-friendly party. Other fun places for a party are a science museum, Build-A-Bear shop, craft studio, or local park. The birthday person should be allowed to pick a favorite or preferred location for the event. Their choice might impact how loose they might get when the event eventually begins.

iv. Choose favorite activities. It is best to stick with birthday activities that the child is already familiar with and often enjoys. This is also the right time for everyone to indulge in all of the birthday person's chosen activities. Even though it is advisable to let the child choose the kind of activities that would be featured in their party, the parents should ensure that each choice isn't time-consuming, boring, or hazardous to the child or the guests.

v. An alternative to treats. Some parents notice behavioral changes when their children consume certain types of foods. High sugar foods with artificial food coloring can trigger hyperactivism, even at parties. Parents can provide an alternative to treats. However, care must be taken not to trigger any undesirable behavior due to food allergies and intolerances, as these can be so severe that it is best not to serve any food at the party. If adequate caution is put in place, the party can go on with ideal meals, snacks, and treats given to all without any issues.

vi. Accepting gifts. Gifts can be the most emotional part of a birthday party. Some families prefer not to open gifts at the party, and bring everything home to be opened later. This can help take the focus of the highly sensitive child. At other times, the best gifts can be perishable items that can be readily consumed there at the party. As an additional activity, certain gifts can be crafted there at the party by friends and well-wishers. The idea behind gifts is to help the child feel special without triggering an excessive flow of emotions.

vii. Celebrate without a party. A lot of families choose to avoid the birthday party and substitute another type of celebration:

- A family trip to a place selected by the birthday person.

- Using the money that would have been spent on the party for a special interest, such as a new Lego kit.

Family birthday traditions spread out over a week, for instance, special decorations for the house on one morning, then balloons in a favorite color on the next morning, then a favorite breakfast on the following morning, a family birthday dance to a favorite song on the next day, and a favorite movie on the following evening.

Chapter 8

Instant Calm for the Extra Anxious

a. How to Calm Down When Feeling Extra Anxious

Everyone has moments when they feel more nervous, stressed, and worried than usual. When these negative thoughts find their way to our brains, it's easy to give in and let them take over. It's up to you, however, to keep them from spiraling out of control. Here are a few tricks to explore in your quest to find some calm right here, right now:

i. Breathe deeply. One of the most operational ways to slow your sprinting heart and make yourself feel calmer is by focusing on your breath. Research indicates that slow, deep breathing techniques can lead to feelings of ease and relaxation, making you feel more attentive, and reducing indications of anxiety, depression, and anger. There are quite a few deep breathing techniques you can try. One popular option is box breathing, also referred to as four-square breathing. Here's how to do it:

- Sit in a comfortable position in a quiet space.
- Slowly exhale.

- Slowly inhale while counting to four.

- Hold your breath for a slow count of four.

- Slowly exhale for a count of four.

- Hold your breath for four counts before repeating.

ii. Employ logic in challenging your fears. Strong feelings of anxiety and pressure come fast, often from irrational thoughts. You might begin to focus on only the worst likely outcome or fall into a chorus of "*what ifs*" that play into your deepest fears. In these instants, try to talk yourself out of it by using reason to dare your anxiety. Ask yourself questions like these:

- What's the indication that this is true?

- What's the likelihood that what I'm worried about will happen? What's the likelihood that it won't happen?

- How will worrying about this help me?

- How would I handle the worst thing that could happen?

- What would I say to a friend worrying about this right now?

Once you answer these questions, you can begin to think more positively and coach yourself through any remaining negative feelings.

iii. Move your body. In most cases, exercise is seen to be a great way to relax and calm the mind, and one doesn't need to do a grueling workout to relish those benefits. Simply taking a walk or doing some Yoga can make all the difference. Exercise aids you in clearing the mind of negative thoughts and encourages your body to release endorphins that lift your mood and make you feel good. Research advocates that physical activity can defend people from going down with certain mental health conditions and lessen symptoms of depression and anxiety. Steady exercise can considerably decrease feelings of anxiety over time, but a quick walk outside or a run on the treadmill can also lift your spirits at the moment.

iv. Chew gum. Gum can help you chase away those anxious vibes. A study submitted that chewing gum can improve mood and reduce anxiety. This is probably because the act of chewing gum rouses blood flow in the brain. The effects can be felt immediately and can aid in the long term as well. Chewing gum can trigger alertness and improve multitasking

v. Take a bath. Research submits that people who bathe in hot water for as little as ten minutes each day have better mental and emotional health. Warm water can also soothe any sore and aching muscles, which can aid in the relief of anxiety, making you feel calmer, both physically and emotionally. A 2010 study discovered that taking a bath on a regular basis can help improve your sleep, which might help you feel calmer in the long term as well.

vi. Go outside. Research indicated that exposure to sunlight can increase the release of serotonin in the brain, which can advance your mood, leaving you feeling more at peace. Another study done in 2020 showed that spending as little as ten minutes outside can improve not only your mood but also your focus, blood pressure, and heart rate. What's more, exposure to sunlight isn't all; being surrounded by nature is soothing, even on a cloudy day.

vii. Write it out. Journaling all your anxieties and worries can leave you feeling light like a burden has been lifted off your shoulders. Journaling aids you in processing emotions in a healthy way and gives you a better grasp of what you're worried about. It can considerably reduce feelings of anxiety. One 2009 study showed that college students who did expressive writing had less depression, anxiety, and stress after two months compared to students who were asked to write without expressing emotion or opinions.

viii. Sit up straight. Your sitting posture can greatly affect your mood. A person slouching would probably hit the wrong mental notes sooner rather than later. By dropping your shoulders from that uptight position around your ears and sitting up straight, you'll find yourself feeling a bit more centered. A 2009 study indicated that students who sat upright were more likely to believe positive things about themselves compared to their counterparts who slouched. Sitting up straight can increase confidence, recover energy levels, and help sack depression. Sitting up straight and tall can also make it easier for you to inhale deep, slow breaths, which can make you feel calmer. Dropping your shoulders will leave you feeling instantly relaxed since it soothes tense muscles.

ix. Listen to music. A 2013 study showed that listening to music before a stressful situation can make it easier for the nervous system to relax once the situation is over, which essentially implies that it helps you control your levels of stress and anxiety, even in tough situations. Calming music or soothing sounds can also help maintain low cortisol levels and relax your mind. If you're looking for instant relief, listening to something soothing might be the answer.

x. Think about what you're thankful for. Taking time out to focus on what you're grateful for can aid you in feeling less nervous and depressed almost instantaneously. Study shows that the best way to do this is to write a list of things you're thankful for and then read it back to yourself. This aids you in focusing on the positive aspects of your life rather than the negative, efficiently pushing away the bad stuff and helping you calm down.

xi. Close your eyes. When anxiety begins to set in, our pupils widen and our faces tense up. You can reverse the trend by closing your eyes and leaving them closed for a few moments. You can give attention to completely relaxing your facial muscles. This simple exercise can help with the elimination of tension, bringing you back to a state of calm.

xii. Play with your pet. Science has shown the efficacy of owning therapy animals. A 2002 study indicated that people who own pets have overall lower heart rates and blood pressure levels and are able to better cope with stressful circumstances. Pets can also advance your mood and lessen stress. According to research, intermingling with your pet for as little as ten minutes can lead to a significant reduction in the stress hormone cortisol.

xiii. Tense your toes and then relax them. Progressive muscle relaxation is a technique that can quickly relieve feelings of anxiety: Gradually tense up different muscle groups and then relax them. It's best to begin with your toes and work your way up. A study has proven that tensing and then relaxing specific muscle groups can aid in boosting one's awareness of their body and tense areas, leaving them feeling more relaxed.

xiv. Completely relax your muscles. Absolute relaxation is a worthwhile practice. Autogenic training is when you sit or lie in a comfortable position and let your muscles go limp. While you melt like a stick of butter, repeat short phrases in your mind, such as "*My arms are heavy,*" or "*I'm so heavy I'm melting into the floor.*" Channel strong feelings of weight, warmth, coolness, and calm as you relax. Give yourself about ten to fifteen minutes of relaxation before resuming your day or going to bed. This greatly works on the mind and body, getting negative feelings to drift away.

xv. Watch something that makes you laugh. A 2017 study showed that laughing regularly can decrease blood pressure, which can make you feel calmer over time. Laughter can also sack anxiety and boost positive feelings. This is widely referred to as *laughter therapy*.

xvi. Smell something calming. In the event where you are near fresh flowers, a quick whiff can help you feel calmer. A 2015 study showed that those individuals who touched and smelled plants reported feeling less tensed and anxious. An added advantage is if the scent is one you love. If there are no flowers nearby, you can try breathing in a calming essential oil, such as lavender. A 2017 research review advocated that lavender essential oil could be operational in treating anxiety disorders and might also improve sleep for some people.

xvii. Focus on a mantra. Mantras are another way of focusing on more logical thoughts and helping us step away from our anxiety and into a calmer headspace. A 2015 study indicated that silently repeating a single word to yourself silences the same part of your brain that makes your mind wander. You can also repeat a calming phrase, such as *"How important is this?"* or *"I can overcome anything,"* to focus more on confronting that anxiety.

xviii. Meditate. A 2018 study showed that a meditation session that lasts for as little as an hour can considerably lower levels of anxiety and stress. You can meditate in the comfort of your home through the help of mobile phone apps such as *Headspace* or *Calm*. Find a quiet space and sit in a comfortable position with your eyes closed to feel calmer.

b. When It Might Be Something More

It must be stated that the above tips are great when one seeks to calm down fast, but they aren't long-term solutions for intense feelings of anxiety, depression, and stress. In some cases, it may be best to seek assistance from a professional to learn how to inhibit and manage these feelings, because if they are left untreated, they could lead to more serious mental health issues. Talk to a doctor if any of these things are true for you:

- You feel like your anxiety is meddling with your daily life on a consistent basis.

- You feel like you have no control over your anxiety, like none of the above tips leave you feeling calmer.

- You've turned to drugs or alcohol to cope with your anxiety.

- You're experiencing physical complications such as stomach pain or a racing heart.

You're having suicidal thoughts or behaviors; you can get immediate help by calling 911 or your local emergency number.

Get the Letter of Intent for Free

Building a relationship with our readers is the very best thing about writing. We occasionally send newsletters with details on new releases, special offers, and other bits of news relating to autism and special needs.

And if you sign up to the mailing list, we'll send you the Letter of Intent E-book, which is worth $35.00, for free. You can get Letter of Intent, for free, by signing up at https://diffnotless.com.

About the Letter of Intent E-book:

No one else knows your child as well as you do, and no one ever could. You are a walking encyclopedia of your child's history, experiences, habits, and wishes. If your child has special needs, the family's history adds a helpful chapter to your child's book, one detailing his unique medical, behavioral, and educational requirements.

A letter of intent helps your loved ones and your child manage a difficult transition when you no longer are the primary caregiver. A letter of intent is an important planning tool for parents of children with special needs (including adult children), and also guides your child's future caregivers in making the most appropriate life decisions for your child, including providing direction to your child's trustee in fulfilling his or her fiduciary responsibilities.

The letter of intent may be addressed to anyone you wish.

This document addresses the following points:

- emotional information,
- future vision for the child,
- biographical and personal information,
- medical information,
- personality traits and preferences,
- habits and hygiene,
- meals and dietary requirements, and
- much more.

Once you prepare, sign, and date the letter of intent, you should review the document annually and update it as necessary. It is important that you let your child's potential future caregiver know that the letter of intent exists and where it can be accessed; even better, you can review the document with the caregiver on an annual basis. The letter of intent should be placed with all of your other relevant legal and personal documents concerning your child.

Found This Book Useful? You Can Make a Big Difference

Reviews are the most powerful tools in our arsenal when it comes to getting attention for our books. Much as we'd like to, we don't have the financial muscle of a New York publisher. We can't take out full page ads in the newspaper or put posters on the subway.

But we do have something much more powerful and effective than that, and it's something that those publishers would kill to get their hands on.

A committed and loyal bunch of readers like you.

Honest reviews of our books help bring them to the attention of other readers.

If you've found this book useful, we would be very grateful if you could spend just five minutes leaving a review (it can be as short as you like) on the book's Amazon page.

Thank you very much.

Other Books by Kathryn Paddington

Have you read them all?

Parenting Children with Autism and Special Needs—
https://www.amazon.com/Parenting-Children-Autism-Special-Needs/dp/B097H8D275/

Made in the USA
Columbia, SC
05 January 2023